A Beginner's Guide to Celtic Mythology

An Introduction to the Mysteries and Magic of Celtic Legend and Lore

Neve Sullivan

Intrepidas Publishing

CONTENTS

Introduction

Truth in our hearts, strength in our hands, consistency in our tongues.

– Old Celtic saying

Why learn about Celtic mythology today? It is often confusing and appears forbiddingly complex, which can be off-putting. At first glance, the body of fantastical stories seems far removed from the everyday concerns of our modern lives.

Existence can feel empty and meaningless without an understanding of our collective past. It can seem as though we are trapped in a vacuum, lost and isolated. An antidote is reconnecting with ancient cultures. By extracting the wisdom found there, we can enrich our lives and rediscover the mystery and wonder of life.

A study of Celtic mythology presents an alternative worldview, one that hints at universal patterns underlying individual challenges. It offers a sense of deep belonging to the earth and each other, and it is an invitation to embark on a quest for the deeper meaning of life. Like a legendary Celtic hero or heroine, we are invited to find the source of our existence. Along the way, we will overcome current parallels to legendary obstacles and terrifying monsters.

Myths and legends are cultural reflections, and there is no right or wrong way to interpret them. There is great freedom in this. When they are viewed symbolically, they can offer timeless insights. We may even find ourselves drawn to a particular aspect of Celtic mythology or identifying with a particular god or goddess. This is evident in the work of creatives, as the lore of the ancient Celts continues to influence contemporary and popular culture through film, literature, and other forms of expression.

Additionally, the recent revival of interest in paganism, Druidism, Wicca, shamanism, and magic has spilled over into a renewed attention to the Celtic religious system. Most critically, concerns over the fractured state of our environment compared to the Celts' reverence of nature make their beliefs more relevant than ever. Their religion encourages us to value and treasure the natural world, and this message should be heeded and honored, especially now.

In our fast-paced and increasingly technological world, many of us feel disconnected from our communities, from nature, and ourselves. To address this, *A Beginner's Guide to Celtic Mythology* will provide a broad overview of the canon, offering a simple but detailed exploration of the myths, unraveling their more impenetrable aspects to tease out universal themes. This includes suggestions on how to adapt and apply some of the ancient wisdom to our lives in the 21st century.

Celtic Mythology: Origins and Historical Significance

The Celtic worldview is aptly expressed by the turn of phrase that opened this chapter: "Truth is in our hearts, strength in our hands, consistency in our tongues." This suggests a standpoint that is deeply rooted in honor, courage, and eloquence, as demonstrated by tales of brave, powerful warriors and the influence of the poet class.

Before the expansion of the Roman Empire and the Slavic and Germanic-speaking tribes, Celtic cultures dominated Europe, including Britain, France, Italy, Austria, the Czech Republic, Southern Germany, and parts of Portugal and Spain (Alberro, 2005). These countries were grouped as they shared a common language and similar religious and cultural traditions.

Although the culture was prevalent in most parts of Europe in ancient times, only six nations or regions in Northwestern Europe retained the tradition over the last few centuries. These are Brittany in northwestern France, Cornwall in southwest England, Ireland, the Isle of Man, Scotland, and Wales (Koch, 2006). Celtic heritage in the form of texts, folklore, and music also survives in parts of the northern Iberian Peninsula, including modern-day Asturias, Galicia, Cantabria, and northern Portugal.

Celtic Mythology and Its Historical Significance

Both myths and legends will be explored in this study, so it is worth distinguishing between the two.

The word "myth" comes from the Greek *mythos* (story, plot, speech). Northop Frye defines it as "a story in which some of the chief characters are gods" (1963: 30). However, this explanation is overly simplistic, as myths do not always involve deities. They can also be about humans, animals, or magical beings such as fairies or giants. More broadly, the term has come to denote episodes that have been handed down within a culture and that are continuously retold or remembered because they have relevance or meaning to that society. Meanwhile, legends are popular, unauthenticated narratives thought to be historical, like those surrounding King Arthur or Charlemagne.

Celtic mythology is best understood as an enigma wrapped in a riddle. It is a labyrinthine world where gods and mortals coexist, animals speak, and magic is as commonplace as the air we breathe. It is a universe in which women wield power with grace and ferocity while Druids mediate between the natural and supernatural realms.

The term "Celtic mythology" refers to the body of myths and legends of the Celtic tribes, and it has been in use since the early 20th century. It usually describes old Gaulish, medieval Irish, and Welsh sources (MacKillop, 1998). This culture's version of paganism originates in the religious practices of the Proto-Indo-European region. We know this to be the case because many Celtic deities correspond with those found in other Indo-European mythologies. For example, the Irish Danu aligns with the Hindu goddess of the same name. Meanwhile, the Celtic Brigantia is the same as the Roman Aurora, the Greek Selene, and the Welsh Arianrhod (Mallory & Adams, 2006).

The Celts believed that, in some places, the division between the physical and the supernatural realms was thinner than in others. This phenomenon is described by the term "thin places," which refers to areas where the distance between Earth and Heaven collapses. This means that it is possible to sense or even access alternative worlds. Believers thought that during the festival of Samhain (modern-day Halloween) the walls separating the two become easier to cross (Leslie & Gerace, 2000).

Most of the Celtic mythology that endured the Roman occupation and other conquests belonged to the Insular Celts, who were made up of the Celtic Britons of Western Britain and Brittany as well as the Gauls of Scotland and Ireland. The fact that any survived at all is remarkable, as most of it was not written down but rather transmitted from generation to generation through the spoken word. While the Celts did have a writing system, Julius Caesar tells us in his *Commentarii de Bello Gallico* that the Druids were banned from using it to record material of religious significance. This is because they believed it to be too sacred to be transcribed.

It was through oral lore that Christian scribes of the medieval period came to write down some Celtic mythology. These tales can be found in the earliest recorded mythic stories of Wales and Ireland, such as those found in the Welsh *Mabinogi* or the Irish *Ulster Cycle*. These texts are likely a mixture of the spoken tradition and fiction created by medieval monastic curators. It is apparent that, in these recordings, the gods have a reduced role, and these figures are often transformed into kings, queens, or heroes while Druids became wizards or sorcerers.

Irish and Welsh Mythological Cycles

Most surviving Celtic mythology comes from Ireland, followed by Wales. Below, we take a brief look at each of these bodies of myth. While the material that survives may be fragmentary, it was recorded in the vernacular rather than the Latin most texts of this era were written in, suggesting that the contents therein are part of a richer national story.

Irish Mythology

The Celtic mythology that comes from Ireland is grouped into four "cycles," which are explained below.

The *Mythological Cycle* or the *Cycle of the Gods* was compiled in the 12th century and contains tales and poems about mythological races, such as the Tuatha Dé Danann, who may have originally been religious deities. The surviving fragments of the text teach us that the chief god was the Dagda (The Great God) and that The Morrígan (The Great Queen or Phantom Queen) was a triple goddess associated with war, fate, and sovereignty. Other gods featured in the text include Lugh, Nuada, Aengus, Brigid, Manannan, the healer Dian Cécht, and Goibniu, the smith and one of the Trí Dé Dáno, or "three gods of craft" (MacKillop, 1998).

In the *Mythological Cycle*, the gods were at war with the Fomorians (or Fomoire), a monstrous people whom the Tuatha Dé Danann defeated in the myth "Cath Maige Tuired" ("Battle of Moytura"). This cycle also contains other mythological works, such as the "Lebor Gabála Érenn" ("Book of Invasions"), a legendary history of Ireland, and the "Oidheadh Chlainne Lir" ("The Children of Lir").

The *Ulster Cycle*, which was committed to writing between the 7th and 12th centuries, originated in a far earlier oral tradition that contains some of the earliest vernacular mythic texts. This cycle includes heroic legends such as that of the mythological king of Ulster, Conchobar mac Nessa, and his court located at Emain Macha, the hero Cú Chulainn, and their war with the kingdom of Connacht and Queen Medb. The longest tale, and one that we will elaborate on throughout this book, is the epic "Táin Bó Cúailnge," known in English as "The Cattle Raid of Cooley." This epic cycle also includes several prequels that tell us about the events that took place before the main action and also some of the independent deeds of the Ulstermen.

The *Fenian Cycle,* otherwise known as the *Fianna Cycle,* was compiled in the 12th century and focuses on the adventures of Finn, a hero, and his band of warriors, the Fianna. One well-known story from this cycle is the long epic "Acallam na Senórach," commonly known as "The Tales of the Elders."

The *Kings' Cycle* includes legends about semi-mythological and historical kings of Ireland. Included are accounts of the origins of the people and domains of the country. One example is the story "Buile Shuibhne," or "The Madness of King Sweeney." This story, first alluded to in the 9th century and recorded in writing in the 12th, is a tale about Suibne mac Colmáin, king of the Dál nAraidi, who was allegedly driven mad by the curse of Saint Rónán Finn.

Irish Celtic mythology also includes many independent texts that exist outside of the four cycles. Some examples are tales of journeys to the Otherworld, such as *The Voyage of Bran,* and others like the *Dindsenchas* (a term that translates to "lore of places") and recounts how locations were given their names.

Welsh Mythology

What we know about Welsh mythology today comes from three manuscripts that were created in the medieval periods. These are *Llyfr Du Caerfyrddin* (*The Black Book of Carmarthen*) dated to the mid-13th century, *Llyfr Gwyn Rhydderch* (*The White Book of Rhydderch*) of the 14th century, and *Llyfr Coch Hergest* (*The Red Book of Hergest*), compiled from ca. 1382–1410. Dispersed through these books are manuscript copies of the four branches of the *Mabinogi*. This is the main source of information about Welsh myths; additionally, it is also the most highly regarded cycle of British prose.

These early texts survive today due to the efforts of the Welsh aristocrat, Lady Charlotte Guest (1812–1895) who had an interest in the early literature of her country. She collected and translated the *Mabinogi* and included these stories alongside several unrelated medieval tales and romances in the *Mabinogion* (1838–1849). These stories were originally written down in the 10th century and survived into the 1800s through 14th-century manuscripts. They are pagan in origin, a determination that is clear from the reference they make to pre-Christian myths and beliefs.

The earliest prose stories, collected under the title of *Pedeir Keinc y Mabinogi* (*Four Branches of the Mabinogi*), are made up of separate but related tales. They also provide the source accounts of several significant characters that feature heavily in Celtic mythology, including Rhiannon, Teyrnon, and Brân the Blessed. Other characters that feature in the text have their origins in archetypes of Proto-Indo-European mythology. Examples of this are to be found throughout Welsh mythology and include the hero who cannot be killed except in seemingly contradictory circumstances and a king of the Otherworld who seeks the aid of a mortal in his feuds (Miller, 1998).

There are many similarities between Welsh and Irish mythology. For example, there are parallels between Rhiannon and Epona, the horse goddess. However, it is unlikely that there was any unified British mythological tradition.

Celtic Pantheon

Celtic mythology is rich and complex, with many deities, powerful female figures, symbolic animals, and magical elements. Understanding these aspects of the culture and folklore helps us gain wisdom and insights into our modern lives.

The Pantheon

There is a large and diverse pantheon of Celtic gods with each possessing unique attributes and domains. Some are well-known like Lugh, the master of all the arts, or The Morrígan, the Phantom Queen. Others such as Sulis Minerva, the goddess of the waters at Bath, are shrouded in obscurity. The list below shows some of the major and minor Celtic deities and their roles and attributes (Falkner, 2020).

Aengus: Irish god of love
Albiorix: Gaulish king of the world
Bebhionn (Bébinn): Irish goddess associated with birth and the Otherworld
Belenus: Sun god
Brigid: Irish goddess of healing
Camulos: God of war
Cernunnos: Lord of the wild
Dagda: Chief of the Irish gods
Danu: Irish primordial goddess of nature
Donn: Irish primordial god of nature

Éire: Goddess of Ireland
Epona: Goddess of horses
Erriapus (Erriapo): A giant in Gaulish mythology
Lugh: Irish warrior god
Morrígan: Irish goddess of war and fate
Ogma: Irish god of eloquence
Rhiannon: Welsh goddess of horses and war
Taranis: Gaulish god of thunder
Tarvos: Gaulish bull god

A more comprehensive guide to major and minor deities is produced in Chapter 1.

Celtic Goddesses

The Celts revered their female figures. They were not mere damsels in distress but warriors, queens, and goddesses who commanded respect and fear. They were embodiments of strength and wisdom—a stark contrast to their counterparts in other mythologies. Celtic lore includes a diverse canon of female characters who are powerful in a variety of ways. Several are warriors, others are wise women or seers, and some are queens in their own right.

Exploring stories about these goddesses gives us a better understanding of Celtic culture. Unlike other ancient European social systems, like those of the ancient Greeks or Romans, Celtic women had autonomy. They could choose who they wanted to marry, they had the right to initiate divorce, and they had sexual freedom both within and outside of marriage. Written and archaeological sources also tell us that the women were warriors, several of whom were described by the Romans. Others were rulers, such as the queens Boudica and Cartimandua. Furthermore, wise women such as the Gallic seers Veleda and Ganna played leadership roles within their tribes, told their people when to commence battle, and participated in hostage negotiations.

These examples show that there is truth behind the Celtic myths of independent and powerful goddesses, which makes the study of them even more worthwhile today.

Animals and Mythical Creatures

Animals held a special place in Celtic lore, where they were prominent and played a critical role in many aspects of daily life. This includes the economy, hunting, warfare, art, literature, and religion. They were not just beasts of burden or pets but spirit guides and omens. Each creature had and still has its symbolism, from the wise owl to the cunning fox. They were so important to the Celts that an intimate relationship developed between humans and animals, leading the Celts to believe that many species had divine powers.

In Celtic myth and religious practice, animals influenced events in their own right. Humans either transformed into them or took on a characteristic or aspect of them. For example, The Morrígan is seen transforming into a crow, raven, and an eel in "The Táin," while in the *Mabinogi*, Rhiannon is depicted as having characteristics of a horse due to her association with the goddess Epona. Several other examples of the role of animals will be discussed in Chapter 1.

Magic and Enchantment

Magic was an integral part of Celtic life. It was not seen as something sinister or unnatural but as an extension of nature itself. The Druids were the custodians of this force, as they were seers, healers, and advisors. Supernatural elements often found their way into Celtic mythology, such as through the use of magic, journeys to enchanted lands, shape-shifting from human to animal forms, and stories about mythical creatures. All these phenomena will be explored in detail in Chapter 1.

What to Expect From This Book

This book offers a comprehensive guide to Celtic mythology across five chapters.

Chapter 1: Unveiling the Enigma of Celtic Mythology explores how to make sense of Celtic mythology and considers the main elements we need to understand to truly appreciate this body of ancient literature. To this end, the first chapter will help you understand the key figures in the pantheon, outline powerful female figures, explore the language of animals, and look at the role of magic, enchantment, and the role of the Druids in Celtic mythology.

Chapter 2: Exploring the Heart of Celtic Myth and Legends delves into some of the fascinating key characters and stories told about the Celtic gods and goddesses. We seek to understand the core themes of Celtic myths and explore tales of legendary heroes and heroines, monsters, and epic quests. We look at how these stories tackle themes of life, death, and rebirth, and we also review fairy encounters and otherworldly adventures.

Chapter 3: Interpreting Celtic Mythology overviews the ways we can analyze Celtic myths to make sense of them. In this chapter, we interpret the meaning of Celtic mythology by decoding common symbols, analyzing themes, patterns, and recurring motifs, considering the power of three, and exploring sacred lands and landscapes to evaluate how geography shaped ancient narratives.

Chapter 4: Historical Crossroads—How Invasions Shaped Mythology explores the link between Celtic and other mythologies to compare and contrast how the myths of other cultures influenced each other. This chapter compares Celtic and Norse mythology, considers the impact of the Roman Conquest, the role of Christian interpretations of pagan legends, and the connection between Celtic myth and Arthurian legends.

Chapter 5: Modern Cultural Influences of Celtic Mythology considers how Celtic mythology is still influential and resonant today. This penultimate chapter looks at how ancient tales have inspired literature, the influence of the Celtic Revival on popular culture, modern manifestations, and how ancient mythological wisdom can be applied to contemporary life.

Once all these aspects have been explored, the concluding chapter will explore how we can rediscover the magic in life by applying the ancient wisdom of Celtic mythology to the present.

Summary

It is important to keep an open mind as you take a closer look into the enigmatic world of the Celts. The mythology of this ancient people is not a linear narrative but a complex web of interconnected stories and characters. It is a testament to the rich Celtic imagination and deep connection with nature.

With this in mind, let us begin our exploration of the rich and diverse canon of Celtic mythology.

Chapter One

Unveiling the Enigma of Celtic Mythology

The whole Gallic people is exceedingly given to religious superstition.

– Julius Caesar, from Gallic War, VI

C eltic mythology is a rich and diverse canon. Myths from Ireland, Scotland, and Wales survive into the modern era thanks to Christian scribes, who recorded them for the ages. Although most of the myths we know today are of Irish and Welsh origin, the Syrian rhetorician Lucian spoke of the Gaulish god Ogmios, and the first-century Roman poet Lucan mentioned several Celtic gods. Celtic myths have also been depicted on archaeological finds, such as coins, altars, and objets d'art. One famous example is the Gundestrup Cauldron, which depicts Cernunnos, the god of nature.

To help you decipher Celtic mythology, some of the main elements of it are presented below. These include major and minor deities, prominent female characters, common real and mythical animal symbols, and magic and enchantment.

The Major Deities

The ancient Celtic pantheon consisted of over 400 gods and goddesses who represented just about everything found in the Celtic world, from rivers to warfare. Although some written and archeological evidence does remain, it is difficult to work out what the use and function of some of these gods were due to the lack of surviving records. What we do know is that most of these gods, apart from Lugh, were not universally worshipped among the various tribes, and the influence of many was limited to several regions or a specific area (Cartwright, 2021a).

Some of the major deities in Celtic mythology are discussed below, including details about their powers, symbols associated with them, and stories or myths where they feature prominently.

The Dagda

The Dagda, who was the chief of the gods, was also known as Eochaid Ollathair ("Father of All"), Ruad Rufhessa ("Lord of Great Knowledge"), and Eochu Deirgderc ("Red Eye," referring to the sun). He was proclaimed to be the "Good God" not because he was virtuous but because he was skilled at many endeavors, including war and magic, and he was an omniscient ruler.

He was the god of fertility, magic, wisdom, and knowledge. He was often likened to Odin, the head of the gods in Norse mythology. The Dagda was the leader of the Tuatha Dé Danann tribe of gods and was considered to be the father of Ireland. He is often depicted as a large, masculine man who had many lovers, including the Morrígan. In other instances, the Dagda was portrayed as uncouth but benevolent. When this was the case, he frequently appeared dressed like a peasant with a tunic that came only to his rump, an effect some commentators describe as comic (MacKillop, 1998). In essence, he was an oafish, good-natured giant who wielded enormous power and influence.

Powers

The Dagda could control life and death, the crops, and the weather. He could also control time and the seasons, as he could bring storms from the heavens and provide rich harvests. He may also have had power over fertility. To this end, he was said to possess two marvelous swine, one that was always cooking and another that was still alive, and his trees were always full of fruit. Such abundance indicates to us that the Dagda had power over the land's prosperity.

Symbols

One symbol of the Good God is a large club that was so large that it had to be dragged on wheels and left tracks so deep that it formed a boundary between two provinces of Ireland. A second was a sizable magical cauldron that never ran out of food. The ladle he used to stir the contents was big enough for two men to fit inside. This vessel, which provided an exorbitant bounty for his followers, was bought by the gods from Murias and was one of the four treasures of the Tuatha Dé Danann.

Myths and Legends

The Dagda is said to have played an active role in Cath Maige Tuired, namely the Second Battle of Mag Tuired, in which he slaughtered many of the rival Fomorians. Even his magical harp, Uaithne, helped to kill nine of his foes. However, after the fighting, he was killed by the buck-toothed Caitlin, the wife of the giant Balor. This story demonstrates that even the head god in the pantheon was mortal. But due to the Celtic belief system, when he died, he would simply have returned to the Otherworld, in which he still resides.

In later folk tradition, the Dagda is thought to have had four great palaces at the depths of the earth and under hollow hills and reigned as king for 80 years (MacKillop, 1998).

The Morrígan

The Morrígan, also known as The Phantom Queen, was the goddess of war, fate, and sovereignty. She was often portrayed as a trio of goddesses, and she is one of the most complex figures in Celtic mythology.

Powers

She could shape-shift into a crow or raven—birds that symbolize the connection between life and death. She could also transform into a fish (she took the form of an eel during a magical battle), a young girl, or an old hag. The Morrígan also had the power of prophecy and was able to cast spells. It was believed that she could predict who could win in combat and lingered around battlefields in one of her avian forms (O'Hara, 2023).

Symbols

The Morrígan is associated with many of the animals she shape-shifted into. Examples include the crow, the raven, and the wolf.

Myths and Legends

The Phantom Queen is associated with several myths and legends. She was thought to have helped the De Danann at the Battle of Magh Tuireadh, and she appeared to the hero Conaire Mór before he died, as told in the tale "Togail Bruidne Dá Derga," known in English as "The Destruction of Dá Derga's Hostel" (Ellis, 1987).

She also plays a prominent role in "The Táin." The story demonstrates her role as a goddess of fertility and her wisdom about the cycle of life, which she passes on to Cú Chulainn. More specifically, she appears several times to the hero as a femme fatale. Initially, she is a lovely young girl who wants to make love to him, then she shifts into several animal forms, but she fails to seduce him in each instance. Instead, the warrior fights and injures her. Later, she comes to him as an old milch cow and, as she is allowing him to drink from her, tells him of his death. Once he has died in battle, she hovers over him in the form of a crow.

Cernunnos

Cernunnos was also known as the "Horned God" or god of nature, and he was a deity of the environment and fertility in Celtic mythology. Often depicted with antlers on his head, he represented the cycle of life and death. Julius Caesar associated him with the Roman god, Dis Pater (MacKillop, 1998).

Perhaps the principal god of the Continental Celts, Cernunnos was the lord of nature. His influence extended to all elements of the land, including animals, fruit, grain, and prosperity. He was portrayed as having a hybrid form: While his body was that of a man's, he also had the horns of a stag. His figure is often depicted in a squatting position and wearing or carving the sacred torc, which the Celts of mainland Europe associated with supernatural powers. In recovered Gaulish depictions of him, he appears with a ram-headed servant.

There is not much historical evidence concerning Cernunnos's role in the Celtic religion and its mythology. For example, his name is only known from one, partly obliterated inscription ("__ernunnos"). However, impressive evidence for his widespread worship exists. He was portrayed on the Gundestrup Cauldron, an abundantly decorated silver artifact discovered in modern-day Denmark and dating to between 150 B.C.E. and 1 B.C.E. Over 30 other representations of the god survive, dispersed all over the Celtic world from Romania to Ireland, indicating that he was a popular deity who was worshipped widely.

Powers

According to tradition, Cernnunnos had power over natural creatures and the wild hunt. This is suggested by the above-mentioned Gundestrup Cauldron, in which he is depicted in a meditative position surrounded by animals, indicating an association and some form of control over the natural world. He was also associated with the energies of physical agility, assertiveness, decisiveness, the powers of wild animals, and knowledge of all earthly entities. Cernunnos ruled the autumn and winter seasons, and, in the form of a bull, he heralded the advent of these periods.

Symbols

Cernunnos's symbols include antlers, animal figures, pelts, serpents, pine cones, erect phalluses, and the sun. On the Gundestrup Cauldron, he holds a snake in one hand, the symbol of rebirth, as serpents shed their skin, and the spring, because they emerge from underground after winter. This also makes sense due to his association with the two cooler seasons.

After the Celtic period, Cernunnos came to be symbolic of devilish and anti-Christian forces.

Myths and Legends

We know very little of the lore associated with Cernunnos today. He was worshipped before the Roman period, so no written account of his myths and legends survives. Some scholars have also suggested that the Gundestrup Cauldron represented priests and priestesses rather than divinities. If this were true, Cernunnos was not a god. Instead, he was representative of a shamanistic practice. However, this interpretation does not stand up to scrutiny, as it seems unlikely that he would have been depicted as a deity in at least 30 surviving artifacts unless he were divine.

Furthermore, the fact that Cernunnos is surrounded by many animals on the Gundestrup Cauldron may imply that he was a form of the Hindu god Shiva in his guise of Pashupati, Lord of the Beasts. This would indicate that Cernunnos is associated with the mythology of this divinity.

Brigid

Brigid was a revered figure in Celtic mythology. Known as the goddess of healing, poetry, and smithcraft, she embodied creativity and wisdom. Her influence was so profound that her worship continued into Christian times, where she was transformed into Saint Brigid.

Powers

Brigid was a healer, poetess, and smith-worker. Her tripartite roles indicate that she had the powers of nurturing care, creative inspiration, and transformation. She also had the gift of prophecy. She had the power of womanly vitality, too, as she was associated with youthful femininity. As a young woman, she was known for her beauty, but in her older form, she was associated with wisdom and was depicted as a wise sage.

Symbols

Brigid was aligned with the triple goddess, so one of her symbols is the three stages of womanhood: maiden, mother, and crone. She was also seen as a symbol of poetry, as in the Celtic period she was worshipped by the semi-poetic class, the *fillid*. Her symbol among them and later poets was a golden branch with tinkling bells.

Myths and Legends

According to the *Sanas Cormaic,* written in the 10th century by the Irish bishop and king of Munster, Cormac mac Cuilennáin, Brigid was the daughter of the Dagda and a female poet and seer. This accounts for the association between the goddess and wordsmiths.

After the conversion to Christianity, a legend came about that Brigid had been the foster mother of Jesus Christ, which remains popular in Ireland and the Hebrides, a group of islands off the coast of Scotland. For this reason, Saint Brigid is known as Muime Chriosd in Gaelic, which translates to "Foster-Mother of Christ" (NicGrioghair, 2024).

Lugh Lámfada

Lugh, also known as Lugh of the Long Arm or Lugus, was the warrior god. The way his name is spelled varies, but he is found throughout the Celtic religions. His prominence is apparent in his having a holiday, Lughnasadh, which marks the beginning of the harvest season.

Lugh Lámfada was a prominent god in Celtic mythology who was a celebrated chief of the Tuatha Dé Danann and the main hero of the *Mythological Cycl*e of Irish literature. He was associated with skill and mastery in multiple disciplines. He was revered for his expertise in arts, crafts, healing, and even war strategy. As Roman influence began to permeate the Celtic world, he came to be seen as an equivalent to the Roman god Mercury.

He was the patron god of skilled craftsmen, blacksmiths, and iron workers. He was also an accomplished and courageous warrior who was portrayed as being youthful, handsome, and athletic. One of his greatest achievements was the slaying of Balor, the leader of the Formorian tribe. After the enemy chief's death, the Tuatha Dé Danann became the dominant tribe of gods in Ireland.

Powers

Lugh had a magical spear called Gae Assail that was so bloodthirsty that it sometimes tried to fight on its own. His nickname, Lámfada ("long-armed"), was not based on a physical attribute but instead testified to his ability to hurl a weapon a long distance or use a sling to do so.

Symbols

Lugh is associated with the sun, the spear, and the wheel (also known as Lugh's Knot or Lugh's Shield).

Myths and Legends

Lugh is one of the three great heroes of Irish tradition, alongside Fionn mac Cumhaill and Cú Chulainn, the latter of whom he may have fathered. Some accounts have alternately suggested that Lugh is a double of the hero.

Much of the god's story is told in the 11th-century text "Cath Maige Tuired" ("The Battle of Mag Tuired"), in which he kills Balor, who is also his grandfather. On that occasion, Lugh comes to the aid of the Tuatha Dé Danann who feared that their maimed king, Nuadu, might not be able to resist the invading Fomorians.

Belenus

Belenus, also spelled Belenos, possibly means "bright" in Gaulish. He was a Continental Celtic god whose influence stretched from the Italian Peninsula to the British Isles, where ancient Europeans worshipped him as a sun god. They believed that he possessed therapeutic qualities and had strong ties to healing springs. Archaeological evidence supports his prominence and suggests that his cult had a significant influence during Roman times.

Several ancient commentators linked him to Apollo or an aspect of this Roman god. For example, a shrine to Belenus located at Inveresk, Scotland is inscribed "Apollini Granno" (MacKillop, 1998).

Powers

The celebration of the calendar feast Beltane may or may not derive from the veneration of Belenus. According to those who regarded him as the patron of the holiday, he had the power to protect cattle, crops, dairy products, and people. In this way, devotion to him encouraged fertility and growth.

Symbols

In Celtic culture, Belenus was associated with fountains, health, and the pastoral lifestyle. His symbols were the phallic-shaped stone, the bull, the horse, and the oak.

Myths and Legends

Like Cernunnos, Belenus's position as a pre-Roman deity means that not many written accounts survive about the myths and legends associated with him. However, in Geoffrey of Monmouth's *Historia regum Britanniae* (1136), Belenus is reduced to a mere mortal conqueror, and a fanciful folk etymology links the god with Billingsgate near the Thames in London.

Lesser-Known Deities

The Celtic pantheon also includes numerous lesser-known deities, many of whom have since been lost to history. Below, we provide details about the powers and stories associated with some of them.

Epona

Epona was the Celtic horse goddess and was the protector of horses, donkeys, and mules. Some sculptures show her with a cornucopia and foals, suggesting she also influenced fertility.

The goddess is unique among Celtic deities, as her worship spread beyond Celtic lands to Rome itself. Roman soldiers brought the goddess back to their capital, where she was the only Celtic goddess to have a designated feast day (December 18). This can be attributed to her association with horses—an animal that was highly valued for warfare purposes. As such, she was popular among the cavalry of the Empire, especially with the Imperial Horse Guards, a royal group of elite riders. Because her worship was especially strong among these leading warriors, and, as kings typically came from this class, Epona may have had a regal association. Furthermore, as a prominent deity adopted by invading armies, she was likely associated with power and prestige.

She was considered not only a protector of horses but also a guide for souls entering the afterlife. Due to her connection with these animals, equine creatures became her symbols. Epona is usually depicted astride a horse or even lying naked on the back of one. Another object that she was closely associated with was a plate called a patera, and she also bore symbols of abundance, like sheaves of wheat, grain, a serpent, or a cornucopia.

In Wales, Epona may have been known as the horse goddess Rhiannon, who appears in the *Mabinogi*. In that epic, she marries Pwyll after rejecting another suitor, Gawal, whom she and her lover later successfully plot to kill through trickery. She is also falsely accused of killing her newborn son and temporarily loses her kingdom until her second husband, Manawydan, restores it to her.

In the Welsh text, Rhiannon is often associated with horses. Pwyll falls in love with her after seeing her ride past him on a white horse and only gets to marry her after she outruns him on horseback for three days. Her punishment for supposedly murdering her son involves sitting at the horse block outside her husband's palace for seven years, offering all visitors a ride on her back. These examples demonstrate Rhiannon's association with the horse form and with Epona.

Áine

Áine, the fairy goddess, was associated with summer and was also the patroness of love, desire, and fertility. According to myth, she had a series of lovers, both mortal and immortal, but beyond her powers of seduction, not much is known about her abilities and symbols.

Stories about her generally talk of her relationships with human men. For example, one of her best-known lovers was Maurice, Earl of Desmond, who fell in love with her at first sight. Having gained control of Áine by seizing her cloak, he made her his bride. The pair had a child together, Gerald, who succeeded his father. According to legend, their son still lives in the depths of the waters of Lough Gur.

Many stories also link the goddess to the sea god, Manannán mac Lir.

Airmid

"Airmid" means "measure," "grain," or "dry measure." Although she was a lesser-known goddess in Celtic mythology, she was revered as the deity of medicinal plants and healing arts. She also possessed extensive knowledge about the curative properties of herbs.

She was the daughter of Dian Cécht, the physician or leech of the Tuatha Dé Danann and the god of medicine. She was also the sister of Micah. According to the myth surrounding her, Airmid assisted her brother in attempting to restore the hand of Nuadu—who had lost one of his arms in combat—after her father had made a silver substitute for it (MacKillop, 1998). She also helped Dian Cécht guard a secret well of healing.

Later, after her jealous father killed Micah, Airmid attempted to classify the magical herbs that grew from his grave. She spread her cloak and laid samples out on the fabric in order of their various healing qualities and uses, and she taught humans about their medicinal powers. Dian Cécht, still jealous of his deceased son, overturned the cloak and hopelessly confused the plants so that no human would learn the secrets of how immortality could be achieved from their use.

Ogma

Ogma was associated with eloquence and learning. In Ireland, he was said to have invented the Ogham script, an early form of Irish writing that was used primarily for inscriptions on stones and trees.

In myth, he was the son of the Dagda and a warrior who was also the skilled patron of poetry and eloquence. He also had the role of conveying souls to the Otherworld. Similarities between his name and that of Ogmios, the Gaulish god of eloquence, suggest that these two deities are related or the same as one another.

In "Cath Maige Tuired," Ogma plays a leading role in the actions that lead up to the battle. When Lugh makes himself known at the Tuatha Dé Danann court, Ogma challenges him to a contest of strength that involves throwing a flagstone over the side of the royal hall, but the god loses. In another story, during the oppressive reign of Bres, he is humiliated by having to do manual labor, such as carrying firewood.

Powerful Female Figures

Numerous powerful female figures exist in Celtic myth, from goddesses to wise women to warriors. Below, we discuss a few examples and their strengths and influence.

- **Queen Medb of Connacht:** Daughter of Eoichaid Feidlech,

King of Tara. She was the independent queen of Connacht, ruling in her own right and not that of any of her husbands, and she led armies into battle.

- **Scáthach:** A warrior-queen who had a school for the training of apprentices, including the hero Cú Chulainn. She appears in the *Ulster Cycle*.

- **Aífe:** The sister or the double of Scáthach and a fighter who was said to be the "hardest woman warrior in the world" (MacKillop, 1998: 6). She was also an instructor and lover of Cú Chulainn.

- **Liath Luachra:** She was a Druidess warrior and the guardian and teacher of the young hero Fionn mac Cumhaill.

- **Macha Mong Ruad, Macha Sainrith, and Macha, the wife of Nemed mac Agnomain:** The three women refer to a tripartite goddess representing the three European functions of the warrior, the fertility figure, and the prophetess, respectively.

- **Fedelm:** As a prophetess, she could predict the future and lived in the court of Queen Medb of Connacht.

- **Rhiannon:** As mentioned above, she was the Welsh goddess of sovereignty and an associate of Epona, the horse goddess.

- **Ceridwen:** This goddess of poetry, magic, and transformation also appeared as an old hag and had a cauldron of wisdom that featured in myths and other ancient tales.

- **Deirdre:** Known as "Deirdre of the Sorrows," she was said to be the most beautiful woman in Ireland, and it was foretold that she would bring death and ruin to the country, which, according to myth, is exactly what happened.

Something all of the above-named women have in common is that they broke European societal norms of the time. For example, Scáthach and Aífe refused to be married and lived independently of men; meanwhile, Deirdre refused to marry King Conchobar of Ulster, instead falling in love with and marrying the warrior Naoise.

While it is tempting to think that society is always advancing, ancient Celtic culture already afforded its female figures power, respect, and even reverence. These mythological entities were progressive, liberated, and remain inspirations for women today.

The Language of Animals in Celtic Myths

Natural creatures played a critical role in many aspects of Celtic life, including the economy, hunting, warfare, art, literature, and religion. They were so important to the Celts that an intimate relationship developed between humans and animals, leading the Celts to believe that many species had divine powers.

In the religion of the ancient Greeks or Romans, animals represented either an aspect of the gods or the mythology of their cults. However, in the Celtic religion, animal iconography is more complicated, with these beings playing a more prominent role by influencing events in their own right. Humans also either shape-shifted into animals or transformed to take on a wild characteristic. Examples that have already been mentioned include how the Morrígan is seen transforming into a crow, raven, and an eel in "The Táin," while in the *Mabinogi*, Rhiannon is depicted as having characteristics of the horse due to her association with the horse goddess Epona.

The Stag

In Celtic myth, the stag symbolized high ideals and aspirations. It was a very powerful symbol and was considered the king of the forest. It represented strength, masculinity, and virility. During the hunting season, the animal's association with the gods of the forest became more pronounced.

The Salmon

As a symbol of wisdom and knowledge in Celtic mythology, the salmon held a position of great esteem. According to ancient tales, eating this sacred fish could grant immense wisdom or even prophetic abilities. This belief stemmed from an old story about a magical salmon that had eaten nine hazelnuts that had fallen into a well of wisdom.

The Raven

This was another revered animal. Known for its intelligence and cunning nature, the raven was often associated with war and death, but· it also served as a guide to lost souls wanting to reach the afterlife. Its presence was thought to be an omen or message from the divine. It was a bird associated with the Morrígan, who often presided over battlefields and deaths that occurred in battle.

The Horse

Horses held significant importance in Celtic mythology. In this context, they represented sovereignty, power, and status. Epona, one of the most celebrated goddesses, was worshipped across the Celtic world, and her cult even reached Rome. She protected horses, donkeys, and mules, and she was often depicted riding on horseback, which further emphasizes the admiration and reverence the Celts had for this creature.

The Owl

To the Celts, the owl was considered to be an emblem of wisdom and intuition due to its ability to see clearly in darkness. One belief was that owls had access to hidden truths that were concealed from others, making them revered creatures with prophetic insight.

The Boar

The boar was seen as a symbol of courage and fearlessness in Celtic mythology because it was a fierce combatant when cornered by hunters or predators. They were also associated with fertility due to their large litters, making them symbols of abundance, too.

From Dragons to Selkies

The Celts did not just refer to everyday animals in their myths and legends—they also made mention of many mythological creatures in their folklore. Some examples are presented below.

The Selkie

The selkie was a mythical creature that existed in Celtic folklore. It was a seal that could shed its skin to become human on land. This transformation symbolized adaptability and change. From what is known of them, selkies were gentle souls who often fell in love with humans, embodying themes of unrequited love and longing.

The Green Man

This was another prominent figure in Celtic mythology. Often depicted as a face surrounded by or made from leaves, the Green Man represented the cycle of growth each spring. He embodied the power and vitality of nature, reminding us of our connection to the world and its cyclical patterns.

The Banshee

Banshees were female spirits known for their mournful wailing. They were said to appear when someone was about to die, with their cries serving as an omen of death. Despite their eerie reputation, banshees symbolized warning and protection, as they provided foreknowledge of impending death so that families could prepare themselves.

The Púca

This was one of the most feared creatures in Celtic folklore. This shape-shifter could take various forms but often appeared as a black horse with glowing eyes. Despite the púca's fearsome appearance, it didn't necessarily bring harm but rather embodied the unpredictability and chaos inherent in life.

The Kelpie

These were water spirits from Scottish mythology that often appeared as horses or beautiful women to lure their victims into aquatic bodies before devouring them. They symbolized the danger lurking beneath seemingly attractive surfaces. For this reason, kelpies were a reminder not to be deceived by appearances.

Magic and Enchantment

In the Celtic world, magic was associated with the Druids. The term is a word that means "wisdom" and is also linked to the Indo-European word "dru," meaning oak—a tree sacred to the Celts. In his commentary on the Gallic Wars, Julius Caesar recorded detailed observations on the customs and religious practices he encountered. Of the Druids, he says (Green, 1997: 10):

The Druids are concerned with the worship of gods, look after public and private sacrifice, and expound religious matters. A large number of young men flock to them for training and hold them in high honor. For they have the right to decide nearly all public and private disputes.

Caesar goes on to explain that the Druids memorized large volumes of poetry, stories, and wisdom, had knowledge of the stars and mythology, and had insight into what happened after death. They were therefore involved in politics, sacrificial rituals, prophecy, and the control of the supernatural world. Notably, Caesar does not make the association between the Druids and magic. In his *Library of History,* the ancient Greek historian Diodorus Siculus suggests that they and seers were different classes of priests (Green, 1997: 7):

Philosophers ... and men learned in religious affairs were unusually honored by [the Celts] and are called by them Druids. They further make use of seers, thinking them worthy of high praise. These latter by their augural observances and by the sacrifice of sacrificial animals can foretell the future.

However, other sources do suggest that the Druids were involved in prophecy and magic. For example, Dio Cassius speaks of King Ambigatus of the Bituriges, who practiced divination and sacrifice. Furthermore, in his *Natural History,* the Roman author and naturalist Pliny the Elder says: "Even today Britain practices magic in awe, with such grand ritual that it might seem that she gave it to the Persians" (Green, 1997: 40).

The Druids were not the only ones who practiced magic in the Celtic world. Fragmentary records also survive of covens of magicians practicing enchantments during this period of history. The Larzac inscription, carved into a lead sheet on a tablet broken into two pieces, was found in a tomb in this region in southern France in 1983. The tablet covered a pot that contained the remains of a woman. On its four sides were 160 words that had been written in Gaulish using a Latin script.

Based on translations, they are an account that describes two rival groups of female magicians. One of these groups had tried to harm the other through magic. In retaliation, the wronged faction then tried to neutralize the evil charm that had been placed on them (Green, 1997). This example shows that magical enchantments were practiced and taken seriously by the Celts.

The practice of enchantment is also recorded in Celtic myth. In the ancient Welsh tale, "Branwen Daughter of Llyr," the god Brân the Blessed and his companions spend 72 years in a state of timeless enchantment before experiencing the joys of the afterlife. They are placed in this state by the song of blackbirds who belong to the goddess Rhiannon.

Also, the story of Diarmuid's foster brother says that Diarmuid is an enchanted boar with a poisoned spine that stands out like spikes. In Iron Age art, dorsal bristles were a symbol of the ferocity of an angry bull. They were used as decoration on weapons and armor to show that the warrior who wore them was as fearsome as a boar, thereby hopefully evoking fear in the enemy.

Summary

In this chapter, we have looked at the main elements that make up Celtic mythology, including the major and minor deities and myths associated with them, powerful female characters, different animal archetypes, and practices of magic and enchantment. Now that we have gleaned an understanding of the major aspects of the genre, we will build on our understanding by considering the elements at the heart of Celtic myth and legend.

Chapter Two

Exploring the Heart of Celtic Myth and Legends

There's something about Celtic mythology which is deep in the soul.

– Enya

I n this chapter, we delve into some of the fascinating characters and themes of Celtic mythology including common motifs, the stories of famous heroes and monsters, and examples of some of the best-known tales. We also consider the importance and sacredness of death and rebirth in the Celtic belief system.

From Creation to Cataclysm: Understanding Core Themes in Celtic Myths

Celtic myths revolve around several themes. For example, love, mischief, and romance feature prominently in these stories, as the gods often play tricks on humans and each other. Animals often change shape at will, and humans frequently shape-shift into other forms. The Morrígan transforms into several creatures, both avian and fish. Meanwhile, when Ceridwen is chasing Gwion Bach, both parties transform into several creatures. Finally, the enchantress swallows the young man after he transforms into a grain, resulting in the birth of the poet Taliesin.

Below, we look at several of the themes commonly found in Celtic myths.

Creation Myths

Most religious systems begin with a creation myth that explains how the world as we know it came into being. However, no definitive Celtic account survives. One may have existed and has since been lost, but no reference or allusion to this has been found.

Despite this, several myths that provide explanations for the creation of the world and humanity have survived. One such tale speaks of a giant oak tree that sprung from the void that preceded Earth, its branches reaching out to the heavens and roots delving into the underworld. This tree symbolizes the connection between all realms of existence—Heaven, Earth, and the Otherworld. Another well-known story involves a pre-Celtic Gaelic divinity, Cailleach, who was said to have created the landscape by dropping rocks from her apron or throwing them angrily at an enemy.

In Celtic myths, water bodies often play significant roles in creation stories. Rivers are seen as divine entities, giving life to the land, while wells are considered gateways to otherworldly realms and sources of wisdom and inspiration. Other examples refer to long-lost cities under lakes, perhaps referencing settlements lost to the sea at the end of the Last Ice Age (Monaghan, 2004).

New Beginnings

Cataclysms in Celtic myths often serve as transformative events leading to new beginnings. For example, there's a Welsh legend about two dragons who fought beneath Britain and caused earthquakes until they were finally released by King Vortigern, a ruler from the fifth century.

According to legend, the king of the Britons had ordered a castle to be built on the River Glaslyn in Gwynedd. His men worked hard, but every night tremors struck, and the structure collapsed. Eventually, Vortigern sent for a boy named Ambrosius Aurelianus, who revealed by magic that two dragons were fighting in a cave beneath the site of the castle. One was the red dragon of Britain, and the other was a white beast belonging to invading Germanic mercenaries. Ambrosius foretold that the red one would win and rise from the ground.

Their battle represents destructive forces but also signifies rebirth through conflict resolution. Later on, the red dragon became the symbol of Welsh resistance against the English.

The Life Cycle

A common theme is the cycle of birth, death, and rebirth, which mirrors natural phenomena like seasons or lunar phases. This link is often made in Celtic myths. These narratives not only reflect an understanding of nature's rhythms but also provide spiritual insights about life's impermanence and renewal.

Before the advent of modern medicine, labor was very dangerous. In the Celtic period, rituals were commonly enacted to protect against death in childbirth and included drinking water from holy wells or wearing clothing dipped in their water.

Birth and its links to fertility and abundance are also common. For example, Macha Sainrith, one of the three aspects of the tripartite goddess Macha, moved in with the widowed farmer Crunniuc mac Agnomain and brought him prosperity by marrying him, increasing his wealth, and bearing him children (Mallory & Adams, 1997). In this respect, her story is an example of the link between fertility both in marriage and the land that her husband cultivated. Her story also refers to death, as she dies giving birth to twins after having outrun all of King Conchobar of Ulster's chariots to honor a bet Crunniuc had made. The curse she places on the men of Ulster later leads to the events chronicled in "The Táin."

Whether it was in the fields, among animals, or of humans, the Celts did not take fertility for granted. The numerous recorded examples of invocations and rituals that sought to increase fertility suggest that it was a serious societal concern. For example, mistletoe was often given as a drink, and Pliny records that it was used in Druidic rituals to cure infertility in humans and animals.

On a mythological level, a common belief was that at Samhain (1 November), the Dagda and the Morrígan came together in sexual intercourse to guarantee the well-being and fertility of tribes and their agricultural enterprises. In some versions of this myth, the goddess had been an old hag and was revitalized by her union with the chief god, becoming young and beautiful once more. This aspect of the myth suggests that the coupling represented a form of rebirth that mirrors the shifting seasons.

Myths were often told to explain variations in seasonal patterns. For example, the stormy days that often occur in late spring in the British Isles—when winter seems to have suddenly returned—are known in the west of Ireland as the "Borrowed Days" or the "Skinning Days." Legend has it that Glas Ghaibhleann, the cow of abundance, also called the Old Brindled Cow or the Gray Cow, defied winter by claiming it could not kill her. In retaliation, the season stole several days from spring and skinned the creature. This story thus explains variations or quirks in the weather at different times of the year.

Voyages to Other Worlds

Other important themes in the Celtic myths were voyages to mysterious and dangerous lands and larger-than-life heroes. The legendary figures experienced all kinds of adventures and often had to perform impossible tasks before marrying their beloveds. Typical cases are the stories of Cú Chulainn and Fionn mac Cumhaill.

Cities submerged under lakes are a common occurrence as well. Examples include Inchiquin Lough and Lough Gur in Ireland, both of which are said to have kingdoms on their rocky bottoms. Such tales are not unique to Ireland. From Wales comes the tale of the Lowland Hundred in Cardigan Bay, while the magical city of Ys in Brittany was located in the sea off Pointe du Raz. Stories about magical kingdoms submerged underneath the water may originate from historical memories of sunken settlements that were covered by the Irish and North Seas and the Atlantic Ocean at the end of the Last Ice Age.

The Otherworld was an integral part of Celtic creation myths, and it is where gods resided and heroes journeyed for wisdom or healing. The various locations of this domain were not exclusive or restrictive, as their human and magical inhabitants could travel freely to the earthly realm and back again. Such travel was possible due to what the Celts called "thin places," where the barriers between the mortal and immortal worlds were thinner or even wide open.

In stories, the Otherworld is described as an ethereal place that is beyond human perception yet linked with our world through sacred sites like standing stones or ancient trees. This reinforces the Celtic belief in the interconnectedness of all life.

The Magic Cauldron

Magic, magicians, and the supernatural played a significant role in Celtic mythology. A common theme was the magic cauldron. Such pots created potions that gave those who consumed them particular gifts or attributes, such as sustenance, and inspiration, or it even rebirthed them. For example, the Cauldron of Plenty that the Dagda possessed was never empty and supplied great quantities of food.

Another example found in Celtic legend is the Cauldron of Inspiration. Ceridwen's cauldron gives poetic inspiration or the power of transformation, so it inspires those who drink from it. Some of her potions can also transform the appearance of others by giving them the ability to shape-shift into different animals, while others give the drinker the gift of *awen* (wisdom, poetry, and inspiration) itself.

The cauldron's knowledge and powers are similar to those of the Salmon of Knowledge, as explored in the story of the poet Finn Eces. The story "The Boyhood Deeds of Fionn" tells of the early adventures of the hero Fionn mac Cumhaill, who was apprenticed to the elder Finn. In the tale, the poet had spent seven years fishing for a salmon that had gained all the world's learning by eating nine hazelnuts, which were believed to contain insight into the whole universe, and that had fallen into the Well of Wisdom.

Finally, Finn caught the salmon and gave it to Fionn to cook, warning him not to eat any of it. However, as he cooked the fish, the young student burnt himself on a drop of hot cooking fat. To ease the pain, he sucked his afflicted finger, receiving the wisdom of the fish as a consequence. Finn Eces quickly realized that this act had given Fionn unspeakable wisdom, so he gave the hero the remainder of the creature to eat. For the rest of his life, Fionn mac Cumhaill could draw on all the world's wisdom by sucking his thumb (MacKillop, 1986).

In a third instance, the vessel is also a symbol of the Otherworld. Notably, the Cauldron of Rebirth, also known as Pair Dadeni, returned warriors who had been slain to life. In Welsh mythology, it belonged to Brân the Blessed and had the power to restore the dead. The body of the deceased was placed in it, and the next day, they would emerge not only alive but in peak physical condition. However, a consequence was that those who returned from death lost the ability to speak (Bane, 2020).

All these myths indicate that the gifts given by magical cauldrons come with unintended and often detrimental side effects. A parallel may be drawn to the popular modern practice of manifesting improved conditions: If this weighs too heavily toward desiring specific outcomes, it may come at the expense of what might serve us best in the greater scheme of things. Importantly, the stories make the point that magic should be practiced with caution and not be abused for selfish motives or in any way that could result in others being harmed.

Heroes, Monsters, and Epic Quests

Below, we introduce some of the most famous heroes (like Cú Chulainn), monsters (like Balor), and stories of epic quests (like "The Táin") from Celtic mythology.

Legendary Heroes and Heroines

The stories of many heroes and heroines are told in Celtic myths. Below, we explore the lives and adventures of legendary figures such as Queen Medb and Fionn mac Cumhaill.

Cú Chulainn

One of the most renowned heroes in Celtic mythology is Cú Chulainn, who was said to have lived around the height of Celtic Ireland's power, so around the fifth and sixth centuries B.C.E. (Monaghan, 2004). Known for his superhuman strength and skill in combat, he was also said to transform during battle, which made him an unstoppable force. His stories are filled with epic battles and heroic deeds that continue to inspire us today. He is remembered as a Superman figure and has inspired many of the heroes of contemporary fantasy literature.

Cú Chulainn makes his most prominent appearance in the *Ulster Cycle*, which tells of how he was born magically when his mother, Dechtire, drank water with a worm in it. The same magical conception story is told about King Conchobar mac Nessa, and the two are often viewed as mythic doubles. Conchobar was either Dechtire's father or brother. Her pregnancy began to show leading to rumors of incest, so the young woman married, but her shame led to Cú Chulainn's premature birth. However, he lived and was named Setanta.

From childhood, it was clear that the child had the makings of a hero. At five years old, he went along to the great court at Emain Macha and challenged all the boys there to combat. Using child-sized weapons, he won. Two years later, when King Conchobar went to Cúailnge, Setanta was left playing. He caught up with the royal party at the home of the smith, Culann, which was guarded by a vicious dog that the young hero easily killed. He compensated Culann for his loss by promising to serve as his hound until a replacement could be found. This is how the boy got his adult name, as *cú* means "hound," making the hero the "hound of Culann."

When he grew old enough to court a woman, Cú Chulainn settled on the beautiful and womanly Emer. Her father, Forgall Manach, did not approve of the match and sent the young man to study with the warrior woman Scáthach in Scotland, something Manach believed to be a fool's errand. While there, the young man persuaded Scáthach to teach him her skills and also received sexual initiation from her and her sister Aífe, the latter of whom gave birth to his son, Connla.

After his trip to Scotland, Cú Chulainn married Emer, and his later career is described in detail in "The Táin," in which he is depicted as the main hero of the narrative.

The events leading to his death commenced after he violated his sacred vow, known as a geis, to never eat dog meat (Monaghan, 2004). Various versions are given of his death, but all refer to his insistence on dying standing. The Morrígan, who had told him of his fate, oversaw his demise, which resulted from spear wounds. As the goddess of death, she presided over his end in the form of a crow (Ellis, 1987; McCoppin, 2022).

Queen Medb of Connacht

Medb was the queen of Connacht in her own right and is one of the main characters in the *Ulster Cycle*. These tales depict her as a forthright ruler, the commander of her forces, and a woman superior in status to any of her many consorts. According to the stories told about her, Medb had at least four husbands, countless lovers, eight sons, three daughters, two children by a lover, and an adopted son (MacKillop, 1998).

In the past, it was thought that Medb was a real historical figure. However, today scholars believe her to be mythological and based on a combination of several deities. In legend, her figure is an amalgamation of the qualities of the goddesses of territory, fertility, and sovereignty. Her character has also been aligned with the territorial deity Mór Muman of Munster, who was associated with the powers of the sun and supreme power.

Stories about the queen say that she could run as fast as any horse and that if a man glimpsed her, he would lose two-thirds of his strength. She also did not age, so she continued to have the allure of a young woman regardless of how old she was supposed to be.

Medb eventually met her end when her nephew, Furbaide Ferbend, killed her. He was the son of her sister Clothra—who had been married to her former husband Conchobar, the King of Ulster—whom Medb had killed. According to an 11th-century story, Furbaide killed her during her daily swim in the waters of Lough Ree by hitting her on the head with a lump of cheese that he had aimed at her with a slingshot. She was immortalized by four texts from the *Ulster Cycle*, most notably in "Táin Bó Cúailnge"

("The Cattle Raid of Cooley"), the plot of which is outlined later in the chapter.

Fionn mac Cumhaill

The hero Fionn mac Cumhaill was a hunter, warrior, and seer of old and modern Irish literature. He is the main hero of the *Fenian Cycle*, where he heads up the Clan Baíscne and the Fianna Éireann. His band of warriors, the Fianna, recalls the unattached bands of warriors common in Ireland in the early Middle Ages. He was first known as Demne Máel, acquiring the name Fionn ("fair," or "light-haired") while he was still a youth. He also bears the name of his father, Cumhall, who died when he was young. His mother was Murna, who may have claimed divine descent from her ancestor, Nuada of the Silver Hand, king of the mythological Tuatha Dé Danann.

Fionn mac Cumhaill had long been thought to be a historical personage, and chroniclers assigned him the death date of 283 C.E. This was assumed to be the case until the 20th century.

The text of "The Boyhood Deeds of Fionn" tells how he was raised by his aunt the Druidess Bodhmall and the warrior woman Liath Luachra. The latter may also have been the midwife present at his birth. These two women brought him up in the forest of Sliabh Bladhma to protect him from those who wished him harm out of envy for his massive potential. It was here that Liath Luachra tutored the young hero in martial arts, and both women taught him how to survive on his own. Eventually, his father's killers discovered where he was, and his guardians had to send him away for his safety (MacKillop, 1998).

Fionn is usually depicted as brave and admirable, especially in stories narrated by his son Oisín or his compatriot Caílte. In such tales, he is represented as the ideal example of pagan Irish nobility: courageous and generous. Notably, many Feninan legends describe his prowess in battle. One example is when he is the only hero powerful enough to subdue the monstrous Aillén Trechenn, who regularly burned the palace at Tara down.

Elsewhere, particularly in folk tales from oral tradition, Fionn may become a crude bumbler. For example, in a widely known story from manuscript tradition, "Tóruigheacht Dhiarmada agus Ghráinne" ("The Pursuit of Diarmuid and Gráinne") he is an aging cuckold and jealous avenger. Another example is his accidental killing of Liath Luachra. He is said to have picked her up to keep her safe while he was being pursued by the enemy. However, Fionn ran so fast that the wind tore through her body, ripping her to shreds and leaving nothing but her thighbones. Devastated, Fionn uses her remains to dig a lake known as Loch Lurgainn in her honor (Monaghan, 2004). Other stories suggest that he deliberately killed the warrior to acquire her crane bag, which was a prize that contained many treasures.

Monsters

Celtic myth is full of terrifying beasts and spirits. Some categories, as mentioned in Chapter 1, include banshees, kelpies, and selkies. Certain of these creatures appear as fully fledged characters in their own right. Below are a few examples.

Balor

Balor is often called "Balor the Evil" or "Baleful Eye." He was the king of the Fomorians, a monstrous race of people who owned Ireland before the first invaders arrived, as described in the "Book of Invasions."

The Fomorian ruler acquired his terrible eye as a child when he saw his father's Druids brewing charms. The result was a basilisk eye that was never opened except on the battlefield. On these occasions, four men would be needed to lift the lid, and it could render an army's forces powerless if it caught sight of them.

According to the story "Cath Maige Tuired," Balor met his end at the hands of Lugh, who killed him when the two met in battle. A prophecy had warned the Fomorian chief that if his beautiful daughter Eithne was to give birth to a son, that child would later kill his grandfather. To defy the prediction, the tyrant imprisoned his daughter in a tower so that she would never set eyes on a man and never get pregnant, thus sparing Balor's life.

However, his greed caused his downfall. He stole the magical cow, Glas Ghaibhleann, belonging to a smith and tended to by a man called Cian. Threatened with death by the owner of the cow, Cian traveled to Balor's lands to reclaim the creature. He then discovered the tower Eithne was imprisoned in and disguised as a woman, gained access to her. She bore him three sons, all of whom Balor threw into the sea when he discovered their existence. But Cian saved one, and this child later became the hero Lugh, who killed his grandfather.

In some versions of the story, Lugh blinds Balor with a spear made by Goibniu, the craft god. In other versions, Lugh decapitates his grandfather and places the severed head on a pike, using the still-potent eye to split rocks.

The Cailleach

The Cailleach is known as the Celtic witch and was mentioned in many Irish traditional tales. Her name, meaning "veiled one" or "hooded one," is often used in modern Irish and Scots Gaelic as a name for an old woman or a hag. It also translates to "old wife."

She is considered one of the most important figures in Celtic mythology, as she was believed to have been a pre-Celtic divinity and featured prominently in at least one Celtic creation story. She is described as an ancient woman with a blue-gray face but has exceptionally sharp sight, although she only had one eye. She was able to see objects and landscapes that stood

20 miles away as clearly as her hand before her. She is also said to have been extremely strong.

The Cailleach was both a heavenly hag and a creator goddess, and many legends have been told about her. One belief is that at Samhain, she would descend from the mountains and govern the earth between then and Beltane, which heralded the beginning of the spring. She was also worshipped as the goddess of the cold and winds, as the Celts believed that she controlled the duration and severity of the winter.

Epic Quests

Many of the most famous stories from the Celtic mythological canon involve epic quests where the hero must defeat a vengeful enemy to prove his worth. One notable example is the "Cath Maige Tuired," the name of two saga texts of the *Mythological Cycle* of Irish mythology. The tales involve battles in Connacht, with the first documenting the conflict between the Tuatha Dé Danann and the Fir Bolg, and the second between the gods and the Fomorians.

Perhaps the most famous epic quest in Celtic mythology is the one outlined in "The Táin," which is summarized below.

The Táin

"Táin Bó Cúailnge" ("The Cattle Raid of Cooley") is one of Irish mythology's most famous epics and outlines the deeds of Ireland's most famous hero, Cú Chulainn. The narrative focuses on a conflict involving Ulster at an unidentified point in the past, perhaps around the time of Jesus Christ (early first century C.E.).

The story begins with Queen Medb of Connacht calculating the value of her assets compared to those of her husband, Ailill mac Máta. She finds that he has one more powerful stud bull than she does, which makes her the less equal of the couple, much to her fury. To make sure she is superior to her husband, Medb finds a better bull that is located in Ulster. However, Dáire mac Fiachna, the owner, refuses to sell the creature. In retaliation, Medb declares war on the land to secure the beast for herself. The prophetess Fedelm warns her that her forces will lose the war, but she is not deterred, and her army proceeds to Ulster.

At the time, Ulster was still under the divine curse that Macha had placed on its menfolk as she was dying in childbirth. This means that the young Cú Chulainn is the only warrior able to fight against the forces from Connacht. The hero demands single combat, and although the queen offers her daughter Findabair in marriage to a series of warriors as an incentive to fight him, he defeats them all. The war culminates in a three-day combat between Cú Chulainn and his friend and foster brother, Ferdiad. The latter had been in exile and fighting with Medb's forces. Cú Chulainn nearly dies from wounds and exhaustion, but eventually, he emerges victorious. The Ulster army then joins him and so they defeat the Connacht warriors (Depuis, 2009; The Editors of Encyclopaedia Britannica, 2024b).

Although Medb loses the war in Ulster, she does secure her bull, which then fights Ailill's. Both creatures die as a result.

Life, Death, and Rebirth—Sacred Rituals and Attitudes Toward Mortality

In *The Mammoth Book of Celtic Myths and Legends*, Peter Berresford Ellis explains (2002: 19):

> Death was never the conqueror, and we are reminded that the ancient Celts were one of the first cultures to evolve a sophisticated doctrine of the immortality of the soul, in a form of reincarnation ... The Celts taught that death is only a change of place and that life goes on, with all its forms and goods, in the Otherworld.

The Celts believed in an afterlife and that it took place in the Otherworld. Existence was similar to what it was like in the mortal realm but without its negative aspects, such as pain, disease, and sorrow. This meant that there was little to fear from death. Instead, it was merely a process where the soul left the body, or, as the Celts believed, the head.

When a person died, the living said prayers to the Celtic gods, and they honored the deities with offerings such as food, weapons, and precious goods. They may have also made animal and human sacrifices as offerings after the death of an important person in ceremonies that the Druids presided over. The Celts may also have believed in reincarnation—the belief that when a soul leaves a body it can reappear in that of another person or animal.

The Celts' ritualistic practices around death indicate that they believed they were controlled or guided by the gods. Examples include the presence of amulets in tombs, indicating that they thought the dead needed to be protected in some way. Notably, Celtic tombs and burial sites often contained many objects, including tools and jewelry. These objects suggest that the deceased person was going on a journey and would need these items when they reached their ultimate destination.

Although many Celts were cremated, it was common practice to bury great warriors and rulers with their possessions so that they could use them in the next realm. They did not know where the Otherworld was or what was found within it, although they did believe that there were many different realms, some of which were located under the sea, some under the earth, and some to the west. However, in Irish and Welsh myths, this domain is always depicted as a land of order, happiness, and plenty.

Laoi Oisín ar Thír na nÓg

The myths of the Celts demonstrate how they viewed life, death, and rebirth. One famous Celtic story of death and rebirth is that of Oisín, a warrior and poet and the son of the hero Fionn mac Cumhaill. The best-known version of this story is Michael Coimin's literary telling, *Laoi Oisín ar Thír na nÓg* (*The Lay of Oisín in the Land of Youth*) composed around 1750. In Coimin's text, Oisín is hunting with the Fianna one day when a beautiful, fairy-like woman named Niamh Chinn Óir ("Niamh of the Golden Hair") on a white horse visits him. She tells him that she loves him and wants him to go with her to the Tír na nÓg ("the Land of Youth") or the Tír Tairngire, meaning "the Land of Promise."

Traveling due west, Oisín slays a giant so that when he arrives in this world, he is awarded with Niamh as a consort. They then begin 300 years of lovemaking, resulting in the births of two sons (both named Oscar) and a daughter.

Eventually, the warrior decides to return to Ireland. Niamh warns him not to dismount his horse or he will find himself old, withered, and blind. When he does return to his homeland, what was once familiar feels strange, as Oisín's old haunts are now abandoned and overgrown. During his journey, he stoops to help some men trying to lift a stone into a wagon. As he does, his reigns break, and he falls to the ground and is immediately transformed into the frail old man his lover had described. His white steed then returns to the Otherworld.

This story demonstrates how old age and frailty eventually come to us all, no matter how privileged we may be. The tale also shows that death is not to be feared and, in some cases, may even be preferable to living for a long time if the quality of life is poor or prolonging someone's suffering.

Fairy Encounters and Otherworldly Adventures

"Come away, O human child! / To the waters and the wild / With a faery, hand in hand, / For the world's more full of weeping than you can understand" (W. B. Yeats, from "The Stolen Child).

Fairies

The fairy folk, often referred to as the Aos Sí in Celtic mythology, are believed to be a supernatural race living in an invisible world that coexists with the world of humans. The word "fairy" is used here to refer to the divine nature of these beings. According to Celtic mythology, they are small and have a winged, human form that can fly. One of the first references to these creatures in the Celtic tradition appears in the writings of Giraldus Cambrensis (ca. 1146–1223).

The Otherworld is often described as existing underground in fairy mounds, across the Western Sea, or in an invisible realm that overlaps our own. In Celtic folklore, it is said that time operates differently within the fairy realm. A common theme is a human entering a mound and experiencing what seems like only a few hours, but upon their return to the human world, they discover many years have passed. This phenomenon has been referred to as "fairy time," and one example is Oisín's experience in the Tír na nÓg, as described above.

According to ancient lore, fairies were extremely protective of their homes and would use magic to defend them. Disturbing one of their mounds or cutting down one of their trees was considered bad luck. There was also the threat of retaliation from these mystical beings, which would range from minor misfortunes to serious illnesses.

Other Creatures in the Otherworld

The Celtic Otherworld wasn't just home to fairies. It was also inhabited by other mythical creatures such as banshees and selkies.

Just as the normal laws of physics did not apply to the Otherworld, neither did the conventional laws of biology. It was therefore home to all kinds of magical and mythological creatures. One example is selkies, which were part seal and part human, and were indicative of an intimate link between human beings and the natural world.

Another example, banshees, were originally a form of fairy. The word comes from the Irish word bean-sidhe (women of the sidhe or fairy people). It was originally used to describe any woman of the Otherworld, and such beings tended to be earthly goddesses, either of the land or sovereignty. However, the deities were demoted to fairy queens when their worshippers were conquered by those of other divine entities.

Over time, the domain of the banshee narrowed until she became the spirit that announced forthcoming deaths. This transformation has been dated to the seizure of Irish lands by the English in the 16th and 17th centuries. Some Irish families, most of whom have surnames beginning with "O" or "Mac," have banshees that signal the death of their members. This is also an indication that they have ancient Irish roots (Monaghan, 2004). These examples demonstrate the survival of Celtic beliefs into modern times.

Encounters With Fairies in the Mortal Realm

Fairy encounters were not unheard of in the Celtic world. They were believed to be particularly likely at Samhain, celebrated from the last day of October to the first day of November. As already noted, the festival was considered to be a liminal time when the veil between our world and the Otherworld was most easily traversable. Notably, both the Ulster and Fenian heroes, Cú Chulainn and Fionn mac Cumhaill, had respective encounters with the Otherworld around this time. As you may recall, this was also the time that the Dagda and the Morrígan mated (Green, 1997).

One prominent example that survives into the present centers around the so-called "fairy mounds" found across Ireland. These earthen masses or hill forts are said to have supernatural protection against destruction by builders or farmers. Today, there are still 35,000 that survive, some dating from as early as 600 B.C.E. (O'Giollain, 1991; Barber, 2014).

Summary

In this chapter, we learned about the fantastical elements present in Celtic mythology. Examples of characters and stories that have survived tell us that the Celts had rich, active imaginations and a strong belief in the supernatural. Their legends also suggest that they did not fear death; instead, they saw it as an extension of life and, at times, preferable to it.

Celtic mythology can be complex and convoluted. For this reason, it can be difficult for us to understand and appreciate in modern times. Thus, the next chapter explores how we can interpret Celtic mythology today.

Chapter Three

Interpreting Celtic Mythology

If you take myth and folklore, and these things that speak in symbols, they can be interpreted in so many ways that although the actual image is clear enough, the interpretation is infinitely blurred, a sort of enormous rainbow of every possible color you could image.

– Diana Wynne Jones

I n this chapter, we present an overview of Celtic myths to explore how to make sense of them. There are many ways of analyzing and interpreting these tales, and there is no right or wrong way of understanding them.

The meaning of the myths has changed significantly over time. The stories of the origin and history of the Celtic people were first told and remembered through oral tradition. Then, in the Christian era, these tales were written down in chronicles and changed to appeal to a devout audience.

Today, we continue to reinterpret the myths that have survived, connecting to the elements that appeal to or reflect modern times. One example is acknowledging the sexual freedom women in the canon enjoyed, such as that displayed by Queen Medb of Connacht, or celebrating the independence of warrior women like Scáthach and Aífe.

Below, we look at some of the symbols and themes found in Celtic myth and also look at the role of geography in shaping the mythical narratives of the ancient Celts.

Decoding the Symbols: Understanding the Hidden Meanings Behind Prominent Celtic Myths

The interpretation of symbolism in mythology is varied and highly personal, ranging from the psychological to the spiritual to the historical. For example, the phenomenon of fierce shape-shifting monsters—some wrathful and terrifying, some passionate—that guard sacred spaces could be interpreted through a Jungian therapeutic lens. From this perspective, these creatures symbolize the gatekeepers of aspects of our psyche that we have to befriend, not resist or fight against, to gain access to a higher level of wisdom.

Symbols Found in Celtic Myth

Symbolism is commonplace in the mythology and religious belief system of the Celts. Common associations with animals, plants, and weapons are discussed below.

Animals

Animals had an important place in the Celtic religious tradition from its earliest identified forms at Hallstatt and La Tène. In myth, it is commonplace for shape-shifting heroes and gods to transform into other species. The Morrígan is one example, as she often transforms into a raven, as is Ceridwen, who changes into many animals during her chase with Gwion Bach, which culminates in the birth of the poet Taliesin.

The role animals played in the Celtic religion can be gleaned from stories written down in the early Christian period. For example, some accounts of the lives of the Irish saints contain references to animal sacrifice. Certain versions of the life of Saint Patrick describe how princes, chiefs, or Druids would gather at Tara to make offerings to the gods (MacCulloch, 1911).

Birds play a significant role as messengers between the mortal realm and the Otherworld. This is seen in the case of the Welsh sovereignty goddess Rhiannon, who has three blackbirds that, like her, are partly of that domain. They are mentioned in the myth "Branwen Daughter of Llyr," where they keep Brân the Blessed and his companions in a state of enchantment that prevents them from noticing the passing of time for 72 years (Byghan, 2020).

Many Celtic myths also describe the transformation of both mortals and divine figures into avian forms. One example of bird symbolism in Celtic myth is "The Children of Lir." As stated in the title, this legend is about the fate of the children of Lir: Aodh, Fionnuala, Fiachra, and Conn. For reasons that will soon become apparent, the story is sometimes known as "The Tragic Story of the Children of Lir" or "The Violent Death of the Children of Lir."

In this story, after the death of his children's mother, a king named Lir marries again. But his new wife, Aoife, is jealous of her stepchildren's relationship with their father, so she casts a spell and turns them into four white swans. They remain in this form and live at Lake Derravaragh in Westmeath for 400 years before fleeing to the Sea of Moyle off the coast of Ireland. They then spend 300 more miserable years there before traveling to Erris in County Mayo, Ireland.

After 700 years trapped in their enchanted form, they return to their child-hood home at Sidh Fionnachaidh in Armagh to discover that their father had died a very long time ago and that the family home had become unkept and derelict. After their sad homecoming, the siblings go back to Erris. Here, they meet a Christian missionary, Saint Mochaomhog, who finally breaks the spell and turns them back into humans. However, because so much time has gone by, the children of Lir are now frail elderly men and women. But as they are mortal again, the missionary can baptize them shortly before they die peacefully and are buried together.

Of particular interest here is the symbolic meaning behind turning the children into swans. In Insular Celtic epics, these creatures are capable of destruction, but they are mostly birds of temptation or escape from the Otherworld. For example, Midir, one of the kings of the Tuatha Dé Danann, disappears in this manner with Étaín after he has courted her for a long time.

People are also transformed into swans as a form of punishment or revenge. This is the case for the children of Lir, who were transformed by their jeal-ous stepmother. The brilliant white feathers of the swan were commonly perceived to be a symbol of purity, which would certainly be the case for four young children victimized by their father's new wife. The transforma-tion of gods and mortals into birds in Celtic myth is also associated with ordeals, shape-shifting, healing, and journeys to the Otherworld. In this case, the children's transformation is certainly an ideal but could also be about healing, as it ultimately leads them to God as their savior.

Weapons

In Celtic myth, certain gods were associated with particular weapons. For example, the Dagda was famously associated with his club, which was so large that it had to be dragged on wheels by eight men. When moved in this manner, it left tracks so deep as to create and represent the boundaries between the separate provinces of Ireland.

Notably, the club was not just a means of slaying or injuring the enemy by using brute force. The Dagda used one end to this end and the other to bring the dead back to life. The weapon was also associated with the god's role as the defender of traditional knowledge or law. He had the title "Ruad Rofcssa" ("Lord of Perfect Knowledge") as "it is he that had the multiform triads."

The god Lugh's "long arm" was a spear called Gae Assail. It has been reported to be so bloodthirsty that it once tried to fight on its own, and it also radiated such heat when it was not in use that it was kept in a vat of cooling water. It was one of the four treasures (or teachings) that the Tuatha Dé Danann brought from the Otherworld, as it came from the magical city of Gorias, which was presided over by the magus Esras.

Irish lore says that only the person holding Gae Assail would be victorious, as no battle could be sustained against it. The weapon had the same destructive power as Balor of the Evil Eye, whom it killed. This example demonstrates that mythical weaponry was often all-powerful in ways that could not be imagined by mortals.

Weapons often included mythical animal imagery. The purpose was to either highlight the fearsomeness of the warrior wearing it or to function as an expression of hope that the animal's warlike traits would transfer onto the bearer of the arms as he or she fought.

Diodorus Siculus refers to Celtic warriors wearing horned or animal-crested helmets to increase their stature and make themselves appear more ferocious to their enemy. Archaeologists have found several helmets adorned with fearsome animal imagery. One example is the artifact discovered in the River Thames at Waterloo Bridge in central London. In another instance, one of the panels of the Gundestrup Cauldron depicts soldiers wearing boar and bird-crested helmets (Green, 1992).

To the Celts, creatures such as ravens, geese, and boars were symbols of warfare. They were often depicted on armor or weaponry to evoke aggressive traits, either within the warrior or to indicate that the fighter had similar characteristics to the represented beast. The Celts believed geese to be alert and aggressive, qualities which were important in war. For this reason, the birds were commonly portrayed on pieces of armor. One example is the goose found on the helmet of an Iron Age goddess that was represented by a bronze figurine found in Dinéault in Brittany.

Another example of avian imagery being associated with weaponry is a helmet from Ciumesti in Romania that has a figure of a raven on top of it and that dates from the third or second century B.C.E. This piece is especially interesting, as the wings of the bird are hinged so that when the wearer runs toward their enemy, the appendages flap up and down in a realistic and unnerving manner.

The Celts viewed ravens and crows as cruel creatures. This association is found in myths where goddesses of war like The Morrígan and Badb could change at whim into one of these forms, screaming dreadful omens and terrifying armies with their presence (Green, 1992).

Plants

The Celts attributed human knowledge of medicinal plants to the goddess Airmid, who was associated with the art of healing. She possessed extensive knowledge of the curative properties of herbs. After their father, the god Dian Cécht, had killed her brother Micah out of jealousy for his son's healing abilities, Airmid attempted to classify the magical herbs that grew from her sibling's grave. She laid each one out on her cloak in order of their curative qualities. However, her father destroyed her work when he overturned the fabric, confusing the samples so that no human could use them to discover the secret of immortality (Ellis, 1987).

Plants also appear as motifs and have certain associations in the Celtic mythological canon. A species might sometimes be associated with a particular god. For example, the healing plant Belinuntia was named after Belenus, the possible god of Beltane, which suggests that healing was one of his powers. Meanwhile, in Scottish fairy lore, rushes are said to mark the mythical creatures' hiding places. The winter plants holly and ivy are symbolically paired together in the Welsh myth of combat between the kings Hafgan and Arawn, with holly representing masculine energy and ivy feminine (Monaghan, 2004).

Analyzing Themes, Patterns, and Recurring Motifs

Common themes, such as heroism, betrayal, love, and so forth, are found across different myths. Below, we highlight patterns and motifs using examples from popular tales.

Heroism

There is one clearly defined age in Irish Celtic mythology from which it derives its heroic tradition. This period in Ireland's history took place around the time of the birth of Jesus Christ (ca. 0 C.E.). It primarily concerns the Ulaidh, who were once the dominant people of Ulster and from whom that province derives its name. The earliest written record of the tradition dates back to the seventh century, but it would have already existed in oral tradition for several centuries.

The heroic stories of the *Ulster Cycle* present a picture of an aristocratic warrior society. The Irish followed La Tène culture, which survived more or less intact as the country had avoided the Roman occupation and remained prevalent until the establishment of Christianity. Experts believe it to resemble the culture found in independent Gaul, pre-Roman occupation.

The primary concern of Celtic heroic literature is courageous action. In the *Ulster Cycle*, common themes include tribal warfare and individual prowess. For example, "The Táin" tells of the conflict between the Ulstermen and Queen Medb of Connacht and her people, all because she wanted to capture a valuable bull. At this point, because the Ulstermen are under a curse Macha had placed on them, the young warrior Cú Chulainn singlehandedly has to maintain the defense of the province.

The hero manages to defend Ulster by engaging a series of Connacht warriors in single combat, successfully holding off the enemy until the Ulstermen recover their strength. Cú Chulainn's bravery in "The Táin" is an example of how the efforts of one hero save the day in Celtic myth.

Similar figures found in other branches of Celtic mythology also display a tendency to save the situation by themselves. For example, in the *Fenian Cycle*, Fionn mac Cumhaill saves the High King's palace at Tara from a demon and also overcomes Dáire Donn, the King of the World. Fionn was also said to have access to all the wisdom in the world after he ate the fabled Salmon of Knowledge. These examples show how heroes in Celtic myth were depicted as exceptional men with prowess and skills above those of mere mortals.

Love

One of the most famous prequels to "The Táin" is "Longes mac nUislenn" ("The Exile of the Sons of Uisliu"). This tale focuses on the tragic story of Deirdre of the Sorrows, who is born when her father, Felim mac Dall, an Ulster chieftain, is entertaining the King of Ulster, Conchobar mac Nessa. Cathbad the Druid casts the infant's horoscope and predicts that she will be the most beautiful woman in Ireland and will marry a king. However, he also predicts that because of her, death and ruin will come upon the land.

This prophecy means that Conchobar's men want baby Deirdre put to death. However, their ruler orders that the child be saved, as he is intrigued by the prediction of her future beauty and decides that he will raise her in his court. When she is old enough, she will become his wife. Conchobar reasons that if Deirdre marries the king of Ulster, no foreign monarch can marry her, and she cannot create war and division in his kingdom.

As the girl grows up, she becomes notable for her determination to marry for love rather than wed the elderly king. She decides to seek out the man she wants and compel him to marry her. One day, Deirdre watches her foster father flaying a calf in winter and sees a raven drinking the blood on the snow. She says to Lebhorcham, the wise woman who is her companion: "Loveable would be the man on whom would be three colors: his hair like the raven, his cheek like blood, and his body like snow" (Mac Cana, 1985: 96).

Lebhorcham tells her that such a man exists. He is called Naoise and was a son of Uisneach. Deirdre resolves to see him for herself. When the young man happens to pass by her, she contrives to meet him on the road. There, she tells him that she would prefer to be married to a young warrior rather than an elderly king.

Naoise says to her: "You have the bull of the province, the king of the Ulaidh."

"I would choose between the two of you and I would take a young bull like you," Deirdre replies (Mac Cana, 1985: 96).

Naoise is concerned about the implications of the prophecy that had been cast at her birth, so he is reluctant to marry her. Thus, he does not agree to elope with her until she threatens him with shame and derision if he refuses to take her with him (Mac Cana, 1985).

Ultimately, his fears were not unfounded, as King Conchobar eventually tracks the couple down to their new home in Alba and tricks them into coming back to Ireland. There, he has Naoise and his men killed and compels Deirdre to marry him. However, she is so unhappy that he threatens to wed her to one of his followers, whom she hates. To prevent this from happening, she kills herself, thereby fulfilling the prophecy.

Deirdre's story inspired later medieval romances, such as the story of Tristan and Iseult, first recorded in the 12th century. "The saga is, of course, one of the world's greatest love stories" and, like the story of Deirdre, utilizes the traditional Celtic elopement tale as its central motif (Ellis, 2002: 16).

Another example of love in Celtic mythology is the story of Rhiannon and Pwyll. According to the story told in the *Mabinogi,* Pwyll, Prince of Dyfed falls in love with the woman after he sees her pass by him on a white horse. He pursues her on horseback, but she manages to outrun him for three days. Eventually, she lets him catch up with her and agrees to marry him, although she is already betrothed to another man, Gwawl, son of the goddess Clud. After the wedding feast, Pwyll foolishly grants any wish to Rhiannon's rejected suitor, who asks for her to become his wife. She urges Pwyll to agree to the proposal, as he will have no choice but to return at the end of the year for the marriage feast. At this time, he will bring with him a magical bag that Rhiannon gives him.

On the occasion of Gwawl and Rhiannon's wedding celebration, Pwyll turns up disguised as one of the servants with the enchanted object. He then requests his boon from Gwawl and that his bag be filled with food, but it can never be filled. When Gwawl enquires why the bag is not filling up, Pwyll tells him that a nobleman needs to tell it that enough food has been put in. But when Gwawl stands up to make this request, Pwyll traps him in the bag and his men, thinking they are playing a game of badger-in-the-bag, kill their leader.

These stories demonstrate how women played a decisive role in romantic relationships in Celtic myth. This reflects the freedom Celtic women enjoyed compared to their ancient Greek and Roman counterparts, as they were afforded the choice to sleep with who they wanted, even if they were already married, and they could even divorce their husbands if they so wished.

Betrayal

This theme is also touched upon in "Longes mac nUislenn." A central theme of the story is Conchobar's betrayal of Deirdre and Naoise's trust when he pretends to forgive them to get them back to Ireland. Before this, the young couple had eloped and fled to Alba, where they lived happily for many years. However, as the years went by, the Ulster king became increasingly bitter that Deirdre had rejected him in favor of the younger man. So, he sends Fergus mac Róich to invite the fugitive pair to return to Ulster in peace. However, Deirdre is reluctant, as she feels that they will be doomed if they go back. But Naoise trusts Fergus, as he knew him as a man of his word. So, they make the journey home.

When Deirdre returns to Ireland with her husband, his brothers, and Fergus mac Róich, they are met by Baruch, who seeks to get Fergus away from the party by inviting him to a feast, which it would have been taboo for him to refuse to attend. With no choice but to accept the offer of hospitality, Fergus sends the couple and their traveling party to Emain Macha under the protection of his two sons, Iollan and Buinne. Conchobar then has his spies confirm that Deirdre is as beautiful as ever. After this, he sends his warriors to attack the hostel of the Red Branch to reclaim her for himself. Iollan is killed, Buinne is bribed, and Naoise and his brothers are also murdered. Only Deirdre is spared so that she can be forced to wed Conchobar (Ellis, 1987).

This example shows how trickery was used to lure Deirdre and Naoise to Ulster so that Concohbar could reclaim the woman he had intended to make his wife from her birth. A similar act of betrayal takes place in the *Mabinogi* when Rhiannon and Pwyll conspire to trick Gwawl so that they can remain married. Pwyll tricks his love rival into getting into an enchanted bag, an act that leads to Gwawl being beaten and killed. Both these examples show the deceiver using a betrayal to either reclaim someone they want to marry or to be reunited with the person that they love.

The Power of Threes: Trinities Explored

The number three was considered sacred in Celtic religion and mythology, with only the number five appearing more often in mythological and ritual concepts. Both the Continental and Insular Celts saw three as significant and powerful, and anything that appeared in three parts was representative of this religious value.

The number was associated with complete cycles: past, present, and future or mother, father, and child. One example of this appearing in myth is when The Morrígan teaches Cú Chulainn about the life cycle in "The Táin." Her appearance to him at the different stages of his journey represents how young and strong he appears at each point in the narrative. In his prime, the hero encounters The Morrígan as a maiden, in the fury of battle, he sees her in her fearsome animal forms, and when he is tired after constant fighting, she appears to him as an old woman. These appearances helped him accept that death was inevitable, even for one so strong and invincible.

The sacred nature of the number may have represented or been represented by a threefold division of social functions: the sacred, the warlike, and the fertile. Each person in Celtic society had a place according to the role they performed, whether they were a poet or a Druid (the sacred), a sovereign (warlike), or a farmer (fertile). This argument is supported by the story of Cesair, who is said to have arrived in Ireland with only three men to serve her 50 women (Monaghan, 2004). As each man performed each of the three functions, such a configuration was possible.

Two common ways in which the power of threes is expressed in Celtic religion and mythology are in the figure of the tripartite goddess and through threefold death. Each of these concepts is explored in detail below.

Tripartite Goddesses

Many Celtic deities appear in triplicate, most of whom are goddesses. Some examples include the Deae Matres, the three mother goddesses of Gaul, and the triple-headed bull of Britain. Across the Celtic world, the three-woman matres were worshipped as symbols of creativity, sovereignty, birth, fertility, nurturing, and sexual union. As mothers, they were responsible for the earth's bounty and so were closely associated with the prosperity of the land. The abundance that the Celts hoped the mothers would bring is symbolized by their depiction on altars with baskets of fruit on their laps and surrounded by acolytes bearing garlands of flowers (Green, 1997).

Other examples of tripartite goddesses include Brigid, Macha, and The Morrígan. Macha is believed to have been one of these deities as, in her three forms, she served the functions of the priest, warrior, and fertility figure. These forms were Macha the Prophetess and wife of Nemed mac Agnomain, the warrior woman Macha Mong Ruad, and Macha Sainrith, who had twins after she lived and cohabited with the widowed farmer, Cruinniuc.

The Morrígan also had a tripartite aspect. She was part of a trio of war goddesses known as the Morrígna alongside Badb and Macha. Nemain is also sometimes considered to be a member, but she may instead be an aspect of The Morrígan or Badb. Another example of a tripartite goddess is Brigid, who has three roles: healer, poetess, and smith-worker. However, according to Weber (2015), it may be the case that this goddess was three separate women or even three sisters.

Gods are occasionally elevated into a trinity; for example, the Continental god Lugus appears to be a triple form of the god Lugh. Archaeologists have discovered three-headed icons at dig sites, although it is unclear whether they were intended to represent males or females.

Threefold Death

The threefold death may have been a Celtic religious ritual or custom, and examples of it are detailed in myths and legends. This is an occurrence where a victim is killed by three different methods in rapid succession. Examples of this motif are found in the literature and folklore of many countries, including Wales, France, and Estonia. Some Irish myths contain a kind of sacrificial death with three components, often either stabbing, burning, and drowning or strangling, cutting, and drowning.

In Irish myth, stories of kings suffering this end are commonplace. Two of the best examples are "Aided Diarmata meic Cerbaill" ("The Death of Diarmait mac Cerbaill") and "Aided Muirchertaig meic Erca" ("The Death of Muirchertach mac Erca"). For example, in the latter narrative, Muirchertach mac Muiredaig is wounded, and then, as he tries to escape his burning house, he falls and drowns in a vat of wine. Similarly, the failed king Conaire is wounded and stricken with an unquenchable thirst, and he is eventually burnt alive.

Sacred Land and Landscapes: How Geography Shaped Mythical Narratives

In the Celtic religion, the natural landscape, including groves, river sources, and springs, was considered sacred and revered as such. The Celts saw the land as possessing powerful spiritual energy and also believed in the concept of animism, the idea that everything in the natural world possessed a soul. This means that, to them, humans and animals had eternal spirits, as did features of the natural environment like rocks, plants, and rivers.

According to Irish and Scottish Celtic mythology, the monstrous goddess, the Cailleach (see Chapter 2 for more about her) created the natural world and its features. According to surviving stories, she created the landscape either by dropping rocks from her apron or throwing them angrily at an enemy. She is also said to have formed the islands off Munster, in Ireland's southwest. While towing land around, the straw rope she had been using broke. This left the Scariff and Deenish stranded in place (Monaghan, 2004). Another tale tells of how she struck an escaping bull with a rod as he swam away from her, turning him into an island of rock in the process. These are all examples of how Celtic myths sought to explain the geographical features of the world and how they came to be.

Furthermore, the Cailleach gave her name to the largest hills and mountains in Ireland, which shows how her supposed role in their creation is still remembered and appreciated today. One example is Knockycallanan in County Clare. Another is Slieve na Calliagh, a range of hills and an ancient burial site located near Oldcastle, County Meath.

Rivers

Some of the natural features most strongly associated with Celtic myth and legend are rivers. They continue to be revered today, and their mythological origins are still remembered and appreciated. In myths, waterways often represented a boundary between the mortal realm and the Otherworld. Ireland's ancient rivers are associated with numerous tales about the Tuatha Dé Dannan and other characters. Their names remain examples of the enduring power and influence these ancient deities continue to wield today. A couple of these tales are presented below.

One example is the River Barrow (An Bheru), which is first mentioned in the *Annals of the Four Masters* written around 996 C.E. In that chronicle, it is recorded as the River Berbha. The name is believed to be associated with Borvo, the Celtic god of minerals and a healing deity linked to bubbling spring water (O'Neill, 2018).

More detailed stories are told about the River Bann, which is one of Ireland's largest rivers, crossing the borders of County Down and County Armagh in Northern Ireland. Its Irish name, An Bhanna, means "the goddess," as does the name of the River Bandon (Abhainn na Bandan) in County Cork. At the mouth of the river is Magilligan Strand (Thrá Mhic Giollagáin), a sandy beach that goes on for seven miles. Close to this is a sandbank called Ton's Bank. It is said that this is the burial site of a storm god of the Tuatha Dé Danann who was later associated with the Irish sea god, Manannán mac Lir. When the seas are rough and there is stormy weather off the coast of Inishowen Head, the locals say that "Manannán is angry today" (O'Neill, 2018).

The mouth of the River Bann is known as Inbir Glas and also Inbir Tuag. The latter comes from Princess Tuag of Tara, the foster daughter of High King Conaire. Her beauty meant that she came to the attention of Manannán, who arranged for her to be placed under a sleeping spell and taken from Tara to his domain, the Isle of Man (or Mannin). Once she was enchanted, she was carried to the mouth of the River Bann and placed on the sandbank in preparation for her journey. As she slept, a great wave washed her out to sea, and she drowned.

In another example, Celtic mythology indicates that Queen Medb of Connacht had particularly bad luck when she was around water. After she left her first husband, Conchobar, he continued to lust after her and took the opportunity to violate her when he encountered her bathing in the River Boyne. An 11th-century song says that Medb's death occurred in the waters at the island in Lough Rae, County Roscommon when her nephew Furbaide Ferbend killed her with a piece of hard cheese fired from a slingshot in retaliation for Medb murdering his mother before he could be birthed. The fact that the Queen of Connacht's death occurs at this site reflects the commonality of this type of demise in stories of the Tuatha Dé Danann, as in their belief system, rivers were a conduit to the Otherworld.

Summary

The examples cited in this chapter show how Celtic mythology is full of symbolism. Animal motifs were commonly used to convey the qualities of the individual to the audience while armor was often adorned with beastly decorations in the hope that their bearers would behave similarly on the battlefield. Myths also tell us of wonderful weapons, acts of heroism, and how the landscape was formed.

We see different things in the vast canon of Celtic mythology today to what the intention was at the time or what the intention was when they were written down in the Middle Ages. The next chapter explores these changing interpretations and how they are related to the many invasions and takeovers of Celtic lands that shaped the culture we are aware of today.

Chapter Four

Historical Crossroads — How Invasions Shaped Mythology

A good name, if you get one, goes on forever.
– from "Sayings of the High One," a poem preserved in the
13th-century Poetic Edda

C eltic mythology is not the only such system. During the Celtic period, many other conflicting belief systems impacted its myths and
how it was preserved. Some examples include Norse and Roman mythology, as well as Christian beliefs. All these divergent ideologies intersected
with the Celts and their religion at various points during the Celtic period
and had a lasting impact on it.

Below, we look at the impact of the Norse and Roman invasions and the
introduction of Christianity. We also look at the interrelationship between
Celtic mythology and Arthurian legend.

Norse vs. Celtic Religion

Origins of the Norse Religion and Its Pantheon

The Norse religion, which has been traced to what is now Denmark, was pagan and polytheistic, meaning that it had more than one god. Old Norse religious views were inspired by earlier Scandinavian ones and may have been related to the solar-orientated belief system that emerged in the Nordic Bronze Age and died out around 500 B.C.E.

It is notable that several Bronze Age motifs, such as the wheel cross, appear in later Iron Age works (Andren, 2011). The Norse religion also evolved from earlier religious belief systems of the Germanic Iron Age people, which likely included the European Celts. According to Tacitus, the Germanic tribes were polytheistic and had priests, outdoor sacred sites, and seasonal feasts and sacrifices (Turville-Petre, 1975).

The most important gods in the Norse pantheon and their interrelationships and purpose are outlined below (Steele, 2023).

> **Odin:** The All-father and head of the Aesir, one of two groups of Scandinavian deities and the primary race of Norse gods.
>
> **Frigg:** Wife of Odin and queen of the Aesir. She was associated with love and fertility.
>
> **Thor:** The god of thunder.
>
> **Loki:** Brother to Odin and the trickster god.
>
> **Freyja:** The most powerful female goddess, the daughter of Njord, and the sister of Freyr. She was associated with love, beauty, fertility, magic, and war.
>
> **Baldr:** Beloved god who was associated with beauty, goodness, and happiness, and the son of Odin and Frigg.

Vidar: Known as the "Silent Avenger," he was the god of vengeance and retribution and the son of Odin.

Týr: God of war, law, and justice.

Heimdall: Guardian of the Bifröst, the rainbow bridge that connected Asgard to Midgard.

Njord: God of the sea and father to twins Freyr and Freyja.

Freyr: The god of fertility and prosperity of the land. Son of Njord and brother of Freyja.

In both the Celtic and the Norse religions, gods were mortal and flawed beings. In the Old Norse mythological canon, this was demonstrated by its stories about Ragnarok, the prophesized end of the world. This was a pivotal concept as it would mark the end of the cosmos and its subsequent rebirth. The final destruction would begin with a series of foretold events, including the deaths of beloved gods like Baldr and the release of the world serpent Jörmungandr and the monstrous wolf Fenrir. At the same time, natural disasters such as earthquakes, floods, and the submersion of the world in water, would be occurring.

Ragnarok symbolizes the cyclical nature of existence, as ruin will ultimately lead to renewal. It also emphasizes that the nature of both gods and mortals is transient and that nothing lasts forever.

The relationship between Thor and the Celtic god of thunder also suggests that the gods of the Norse and the Celtic pantheon have a joint source. The name "Taranis" means "thunderer" and is likely related to that of Thor, which has the same meaning. In Norse mythology, the mother of Thor is Fjörgyn, whose name is equivalent to that of the thunder gods of other Indo-European cultures and is associated with the oak tree, which is a species that was sacred in the Celtic belief system. Notably, Cassius Maximus Tyrius tells us that the Celts venerated their counterpart to Jupiter (the Roman god of thunder) not with statues but by worshipping these trees, indicating that Thor and Taranis had a common origin (Chadwick, 1900).

Relationship Between the Norse and Celtic Religions

There was a great deal of cultural exchange between the Celts and their Scandinavian contemporaries. Between the 8th and 11th centuries, Norsemen traveled to the British Isles, where they were known as Vikings. Here, they raided, conquered, settled, and traded. By the start of the medieval period, their kingdoms had developed trade links reaching as far south as southern Europe and the Mediterranean and westward to Ireland and Britain (Blair, 2003).

The earliest recorded Viking raids, the first of which took place in 789 C.E., targeted Christian monasteries, which were often situated in isolated locations that made them vulnerable to attack. Initially, the Norsemen's activity in the British Isles consisted of similar raids and trade, but from 865 to 1066, they saw Britain as a place for potential colonization, so they conquered land and established settlements there. The best-known example is the Danelaw area of northern England, which was under Viking control during this period.

The Norse invaders carried their religion over to the places they conquered. In the 870s, Norwegian settlers colonized Iceland and brought their beliefs with them. The names of certain sites suggest that Thor was the most popular deity in this country, while the sagas show that worshippers of Freyr also lived there, including a priest who was devoted to the god and who appeared in the later *Hrafnkels Saga*. No such names relating to Odin have been found, suggesting he was not as popular there as some of the other gods. Notably, the Old Norse religion and Christianity coexisted peacefully in Iceland in the ninth century.

Viking settlers also brought the pre-Christian Scandinavian religion to Britain in the later 800s (Jolly, 1996). Possible religious sites are indicated by the names given to these locations. For example, Roseberry Topping in North Yorkshire was known as Othensberg in the 12th century, which comes from Óðinsberg, meaning "Hill of Odin." Several other English place names contain Old Norse references to religious elites, including *álfr*, *skratii*, and *troll*. Notably, all these terms refer to creatures that appear in Norse myth.

Significant cultural exchange between the Norsemen and the Celts meant that their religions shared several common characteristics; however, these were likely related to the common Germanic origin of their ideologies rather than the trading of customs that took place after the Viking invasions.

The Roman Conquest and Its Impact on Indigenous Beliefs

In 59 B.C.E., the Roman senate appointed Julius Caesar as the governor of southern Gaul (modern-day France). He immediately began a series of campaigns to conquer the territory and finally completed the task in 50 B.C.E. Caesar wrote an account of his military campaigns in his commentary on the Gallic Wars, titled *Commentarii de Bello Gallico*, where he also made note of the Gaul's customs and religious practices he witnessed. In his text, he presents a comprehensive account of the Celts' religious system and the prominent role the Druids played in Gallic society. He says this about their religious beliefs in *Gallic Wars, VI*, 13-14 (Green, 1997: 10):

> They are chiefly anxious to have men believe the following: that souls do not suffer death, but after death pass from one body to another; and they regard this as the strongest incentive to valor since the fear of death is disregarded.

Caesar then goes on to describe the gods the local people worshipped in *Gallic Wars, VI* 16-17 (Green, 1997: 23):

Of the gods they most of all worship Mercury. He has the largest number of images, and they regard him as the inventor of all the arts, as their guide on the roads and in travel, and as chiefly influential in making money and in trade. Next to him, they worship Apollo, Mars, Jupiter, and Minerva. About the gods, they hold nearly the same views that other people do: That Apollo drives away disease, that Minerva first instituted the arts and crafts, that Jupiter rules the heavens, and Mars the issue of war.

From this passage, it is clear that the Romans had a strong interest in the gods the Celts worshipped and why they were revered. However, Caesar Romanizes the deities, giving them the names of their counterparts instead of referring to them by those the Gauls would have used. This was most likely a practical decision to make it easier for the other Roman citizens whom he was writing for so that they would understand which gods he was referring to. The problem with this is that it makes it harder for contemporary historians to work out the Celtic equivalents Caesar encountered as Governor of Gaul.

The Romans did not attempt to gain a foothold in Britain until a century later. In 43 C.E., Emperor Claudius began the conquest of Britain in earnest. By 87 C.E., the Romans had taken over the majority of the southern half of Britain, namely, most of England and Wales. This became the province of Britannia. However, their attempts to take hold of Scotland and Ireland were unsuccessful (Alcock, 2011).

Romano-Celtic Gods

Invader influence led to substantial changes in Celtic culture but did not suppress it and its traditions. Instead, a dynamic and exciting hybrid emerged. The Romanization of the Celtic religion led to the emergence of deities such as Apollo Grannus, Lenus Mars, and Telesphorus. These figures combined characteristics of divine beings from both belief systems.

As the Roman Empire expanded, knowledge of their gods and those of the people they had conquered spread across the ancient world. For example, all of the sun god archetypes—from the Mediterranean to North America to Central Europe—began to merge through religious syncretism, amalgamating to form one single deity, the god Apollo. Around the first century C.E., the Celts adopted Roman forms of expression while also retaining their names for deities in occasional acts of traditional worship.

By the second century C.E., Roman names for gods became more popular due to a decline in the Celtic side of the hybrid religion. This may have been linked to the replacement of the Celtic language with Latin, especially among the upper echelons of Celtic society. Significantly, by the fourth century, most references to deities in Gaul were by their Roman names rather than their Celtic equivalents (King, 1990). This is an indication that throughout hundreds of years, the Romano-Celtic religion became a regional variant of the Empire's cults.

Information about Celtic deities and how they were worshipped survived from the Roman period. Some evidence includes images and inscribed dedications that have been found across the Celtic parts of Europe. We also have acquired knowledge of the Celtic gods and goddesses of Gaul thanks to Caesar's history of the war in Gaul, the aforementioned *Commentarii de Bello Gallico*. He mentions the five principal gods worshipped in the domain and gives them the names of the closest equivalent Roman gods. He also describes their roles in Celtic myth and culture (Green, 1997).

According to Caesar, Mercury was the most venerated of all the Celtic deities, something that is proven by the fact that numerous representations of him have been discovered. He was seen as the originator of the arts, the supporter of trade and adventurers, and the primary decider of commerce and profit. The Gauls also revered Apollo, Mars, Jupiter, and Minerva, and they held equal importance across the Celtic world. Apollo cured sickness. Healing cults were associated with him in his native guises of Belenus, Moritasgus, and Grannus. The sects dedicated to him were very prominent in Romano-Celtic Gaul. Meanwhile, the sky god Jupiter was equated with the indigenous solar and thunder gods. Similarly, Minerva encouraged skills development, and Mars informed the outcome of welfare.

Acquirement and Adaption of Celtic Religious Practices

It appears that as well as influencing Celtic religious practices, the Romans also acquired and adapted them. In at least one instance, the Romans even adopted and devoted themselves to Celtic gods, as was the case with the horse goddess Epona. The Imperial Horse Guards, a royal group of elite riders, worshipped her and brought her cult to Rome, where she was given a designated feast day on December 18. See Chapter 1 for further details.

Another important example was the veneration of water as a source of healing. The Celts often used water for curative purposes, believing pure spring water could heal disease and provide physical and spiritual purification (Green, 1989).

Springs were the main focus of cult practices during the Romano-Celtic period, but these sites may have been venerated before the Roman occupation. According to historians, it is likely that Gaulish springs were venerated in the Neolithic and Bronze Ages. Similar aquatic sources like that at Duchcov, a small town in the Czech Republic, date back to the very early Iron Age. However, around the end of the Celtic period and the beginning of the Romano-Celtic era, there was a dramatic increase in religious practices around sacred springs that were believed to cure illness.

During the Romano-Celtic period, shrines were established at sacred springs and were visited by a large number of pilgrims. One example is the cult of Sulis Minerva at Bath (formerly known as Aqua Sulis), which honored the healer and goddess of retribution. She was worshipped at the town's magnificent bath complex that the Romans built around the natural hot springs. Following Boudica's revolt in the 60s and 70s C.E., the Roman Baths were constructed with funding from the Empire and through the organization of the army in the area. Their creation is reflective of a combination of Roman technological skill and Gallic workmanship.

However, it is important to acknowledge that religious interest in the springs pre-dates the Roman period, as Celtic coins traced to the early first century C.E. have been recovered from the King's Bath Spring and the name "Sulis" relates to the Suleviae, a Celtic triad originally worshipped in Germany (Irby-Massie, 1999).

The Influence of Christian Interpretations on Pagan Legends

Conversion of the British to Christianity

Between the third and fifth centuries C.E., which marked the end of the Roman period, Europe slowly converted to Christianity, leading to the decline of the Celtic religion. This began in the fourth century and, by the fifth, only remote shrines to the Romano-Celtic gods survived on the continent. However, Britain took longer to embrace the new faith. The process of the mass conversion to Christianity only took off in the sixth century when a small group of missionaries crossed the channel to bring their belief system to Kent. At the time, other teachers were already active in the west of Britain. Before long, the temples of the pagan gods had been replaced with little churches and carved crosses erected in honor of the single Christian God.

The conversion of the English is recorded in detail by Bede in his *Ecclesiastical History of the English People* (ca. 731). His account suggests that conversion to Christianity was a long, drawn-out process and far from clear-cut. The first of the five books that make up the *Ecclesiastical History* presents a brief account of the faith in Roman Britain, including the martyrdom of Saint Alban and the story of Augustine's mission to England in 597, which brought Christianity to the land (Campbell, 2004).

The second book follows the continued progression of the religion in Kent and the first attempts to evangelize Northumbria. Notably, Bede thought that the British played very little part in the conversion of their own country. He makes no mention of any native British contribution to the process in Northumbria, either from within the kingdom or outside of it. He claimed that: "To other unspeakable crimes, which Gildas, their [the British's] own historian describes in doleful words, was added this crime, that they never preached the faith to the Saxons or Angles who inhabited Britain with them" (Rollaston, 2003: 119).

Here, the ancient scholar seems to attack the British for not being evangelistic enough in their faith and for being too respectful of the beliefs of others. In his Christian zeal, Bede was unable to see how people of different faiths could live alongside each other while respecting and cherishing their differences. He goes on to claim that the British would be punished for their failure to convert their neighbors. In the second book of his *Ecclesiastical History*, he records how Aethelfrith, the ruler of the Anglo-Saxon kingdom of Bernicia, defeated the British army and slaughtered the clergy at Chester. He suggests this was a divine punishment for their lack of fervor.

Also in the second book, Bede recalls how the Christian cause in Britain experienced a setback when Penda, the pagan king of Mercia, killed the newly converted Edwin of Northumbria at the Battle of Hatfield Chase in about 632. However, in this instance, the evangelization of King Edwin and that of another Northumbrian ruler, Oswald, failed to save either from defeat by the pagan king.

This setback proved to be temporary, as in the third book, Bede presents an account of the Synod of Whitby, a major turning point in English ecclesiastical history. This aligned the English church with Rome rather than the customs of the Irish monks at Iona. The fourth book begins with an account of Wilfrid's efforts to bring Christianity to the kingdom of Sussex, and the fifth brings the reader to Bede's day and implies that Christianity is still not fully established in England, partly on account of the British church still being in conflict over the correct day of Easter (Farmer, 1978).

These examples demonstrate how England's journey from being a pagan to becoming a Christian country was an arduous, centuries-long process with no obvious beginning or end date.

Merging of Christian Saints With Pagan Gods

Just because Britain had become an evangelized country does not mean that it had entirely separated itself from its pagan past. Oral lore and tradition preserved many Celtic myths and legends, ensuring that these tales survived the Roman occupation and the conversion to Christianity. From the seventh century onward, these stories were written down, although, by this point, they had lost their original religious meaning. Some evidence also suggests that some of the Christians who transcribed early Irish and Welsh texts were hostile to pagan traditions and removed material they considered offensive to their belief system.

In their texts, these scribes often reduced the role of the gods or transformed them from deities into kings, queens, or heroes; meanwhile, Druids were presented as wizards or sorcerers. One example is Conchobar mac Nessa, the King of Ulster, who may have originally been a god, and Rhiannon, who was the Welsh goddess of sovereignty and equivalent to Epona. Also, Lugh Lambfada was changed into Lugh-Chromain ("Stooping Lugh") or "leprechaun" in modern English. This interference therefore changed the most senior of the Celtic gods into a ridiculous imaginary creature.

However, such disrespect for old Celtic stories was far from universal. For example, in the seventh century, an oral tradition of native heathen lore and literature was charmingly transcribed in the little monastery of Drumsnat in County Monaghan in the north of Ireland, forming the content of the earliest Irish manuscript of which we know—the *Cín Dromma Snechtai*. This volume contained the stories and poems of the god Midir, a son of the Dagda who appears in several mythological stories. It has been observed that (Chadwick, 1960: 158):

It can surely be no accident that these heathen traditions are the earliest to be written down and must have been handed directly from the Age of the Saints; but indeed, the Irish monastic church never turned a cold shoulder on its ancient secular tradition, but lovingly collected them in great vellum books, so large that they are almost libraries themselves.

The lingering affection even monks showed for oral pagan traditions suggests that they were keen to retain them in some way shape or form, even if they no longer subscribed to the Celtic belief system.

An interesting aspect of Britain's conversion to Christianity is the syncretism of the two religions, which included the process of merging Christian saints with pagan gods. As part of this process, festivals were reimagined as parts of the Christian calendar. To this end, Samhain was transformed into All Hallows' Day, All Saints' Day, and All Souls' Day, celebrated on October 31, November 1, and November 2, respectively.

Regarding the merging of Christian saints and pagan gods, after Ireland converted to Christianity in 453 C.E., the church transformed the goddess Brigid into a Christian saint. She was the patroness of farm work and cattle and was believed to protect households from fire and catastrophe. This example shows how, as a pre-eminent religious figure, she retained the pastoral function she had as a goddess. Her feast day is February 1—this had been the date of the pagan festival Imbolc, which marked the beginning of spring.

Some traditions associated with Saint Brigid hint at her high status in the Celtic pantheon. For example, one tradition from the Hebrides has it that she was the foster mother of Christ. Women in this role were honored and revered in Celtic society. They were considered more important than the natural parents, and their relationship with their foster children was perceived as sacred (NicGrioghair, 2024).

The transformed-goddess-to-saint story also overlapped with that of Brigid of Kildare, who, alongside Patrick and Columba, is one of the three patron saints of Ireland. She is thought to have been born in the mid-fifth century at Faughart, north of Dundalk in County Louth, and as an abbess, she founded a religious house at Kildare, where she died in 525 (MacKillop, 1998). The symbol of her sanctuary was a serpent, which is also one of the symbols of the goddess of the same name. As this historical figure is an obscure one, it is easy to combine her story with that of the far-better-known Celtic goddess and later saint.

The Connection Between Arthurian Legends and Celtic Myths: Debating Their Origins

Origins of Arthurian Legend

There is a strong connection between Arthurian legends and Celtic myths. Some of the most famous tales from Western Europe are those about the king and his knights. The ninth-century historian Nennius tells of a Celtic king of Britain named Arthur, who rallied his fellow men and fought against the Germanic Saxon invaders sometime in the early Christian era, approximately around the sixth century. References to the same or a similar figure also appear in the Welsh annals.

Other sources also indicate that Arthur was a real historical figure. According to historian John Morris, the oldest reference to the legendary ruler is found in an epitaph honoring the memory of a warrior who died around 80 years after Arthur's time. The poet praises the warrior's prowess but adds "Still, he was no Arthur" (Morris, 1973: 116). Furthermore, when the last lowland British armies were destroyed in the middle of the seventh century, they were remembered as "the heirs of great Arthur" (Morris, 1973: 116). These references suggest that Arthur was a famous commander of the past. Morris adds that "Artorius" was a common Roman name, implying that the historical figure was a commander from a wealthy Romano-Celtic background.

This evidence and Nennius's account suggest that there was some historical reality behind King Arthur and the stories told about him. However, others such as historian Marc Morris argue that King Arthur never existed. Instead, he suggests that the hero began life as an elemental figure or demigod. Medieval writers then took this legendary superhuman figure and turned him into a real person. In the early ninth century, Nennius did this when he wrote Arthur into his account of the struggle between the Britons and the Anglo-Saxon invaders.

Nennius's version of the man was shadowy and obscure, but Arthur underwent a dramatic reimagining in the 1130s when a mischievous Oxford scholar called Geoffrey of Monmouth wrote the mainly fictitious *The History of the Kings of Britain*. Geoffrey made the king the greatest of all the Britons and a one-time ruler of the whole world. He tells of how he had taken the throne at the age of just 15, ruled over the entirety of Britain, and won many battles. Eventually, he was mortally wounded at the Battle of Camblan against Mordred, following which he traveled to the Isle of Avalon to die. According to the text, this death occurred in 542 C.E. (Geoffrey of Monmouth, 1966).

Not everyone believed that Geoffrey's *History* was genuine. For example, in the 1180s, William of Newburgh wrote: "Everything this man wrote about Arthur and his successors, and indeed his predecessors ... was made up!" (Morris, 2008: 163). But it was too late to dismiss the scholar's version of events out of hand, as his text was a medieval bestseller. This is proven by the 215 manuscript copies that survive today—the only book that has more surviving medieval manuscripts is the Bible (Morris, 2008).

As a result of the popularity of *The History of the Kings of Britain,* other writers wrote about Arthur and embellished his myth. To this end, the famed king soon acquired a castle called Camelot, a host of knightly companions, and the Round Table. It is apparent that most of the story of the legend is made up. What remains unclear is whether he was originally a god or a man. Regardless, he was a Celtic figure, either a minor king or a deity.

The Connection Between Arthurian Legend and Celtic Myth

Several elements found in Arthurian legends hark back to Celtic myth. Such themes include the power of the goddess of sovereignty, without whose approving presence a king's right to rule was in jeopardy. Another example is the love triangle between a queen and her two lovers, as expressed in Arthurian legend by the romantic conflict between Guinevere, Arthur, and Lancelot. This example can be understood as a human reflection of the myth of the goddess who marries one king after another. Similarly, John Grigsby (2002) proposes that the witch Morgan le Fay, Arthur's half-sister, is a mythic version of The Morrígan, the Irish war goddess.

Another example is the story of the Fisher King. When the ruler is wounded in his phallus, he is unmanned, and his land becomes barren. This reflects how, in the Celtic framework, a blemished monarch finds no favor with the land's goddesses. Thus, although not part of the Celtic religion, the tales of Camelot and the Knights of the Round Table form an important cultural expression of Celtic ideas and ideals.

Historians have also found evidence that suggests that there was a link between the King Arthur of medieval myth and a pre-Christian Celtic deity. According to the writer L. Sprague de Camp (1964), the Celts worshipped a god called Artur in Ireland and Artaius in Gaul. The name may be connected by the words "to plow" (*arare* in Latin), which would mean that Arthur was originally the god of agriculture. Alternatively, the name may come from the Greek *arktos* which means "bear," making him a bear god, or even "black," suggesting he was the god of ravens. Another suggestion for the origin of the name Arthur is Artor, "the plowman," as *ar du* is Welsh for the "dark-plowed earth" and *ard dhu* is Gaelic for "the dark one" (Murray, 2013).

Those who promote the idea that King Arthur was originally a Celtic god suggest that the Celts originally viewed him as a force of nature. According to Elizabeth Jenkins, his myth maintained an "extraordinary power" over the minds of the Celtic people, as they saw him all across the natural world, on hillsides, caves, boulders, and streams, several of which bore his name. They also saw him in the sky, as the Great Bear constellation of stars was known as "Arthur's Wain," and Arcturus was the fastest moving of all the brighter stars (Jenkins, 1990).

The Celts may have even named the wind after the hero, as implied by the lines from the following ancient verse: Arthur o'Bower has broken his band / And he comes roaring up the land; / [He was] leader of the Ride of the Dead, who collects the souls and rides with them through the air at night (Murray, 2013: 1).

These examples suggest that King Arthur was originally a minor Celtic deity who later evolved into a mythological king.

Summary

The evidence presented in this chapter shows that Celtic myth did not exist in isolation, as it shared its origins with other pagan Germanic belief systems, such as Old Norse mythology. However, Viking paganism survived longer than the Celtic belief system and existed alongside the Christianity of the people the Scandinavians conquered or neighbored in the eighth and ninth centuries. The Celts' beliefs were also informed by the Romans after their conquests of the Gauls and parts of Britain, as the Celts adopted the names of the Roman gods and the invaders expanded existing cults, such as the one to Sulis Minerva at Bath.

It is also apparent that Celtic myth and legend were manipulated and altered by Christian scribes after the advent of Christianity when these stories were finally written down in the medieval period. Celtic myth also informed other legends created in the Middle Ages, such as the tale of King

Arthur, who was either a commander during the Roman period or could have been a minor Celtic deity.

These examples show that Celtic mythology had a profound influence on other stories and belief systems. It is also clear that it continues to influence and inform us today. This is the focus of the next chapter.

Chapter Five

Modern Cultural Influences of Celtic Mythology

For a while, the hobbits continued to talk and think of the past journey and of the perils that lay ahead; but such was the virtue of the land of Rivendell that soon all fear and anxiety was lifted from their minds. The future, good or ill, was not forgotten but ceased to have any power over the present. Health and hope grew strong in them, and they were content with each good day as it came, taking pleasure in every meal, and in every word and song.

– J. R. R. Tolkien, from The Fellowship of the Ring

Why should we bother to continue learning about Celtic mythology? Yes, it contains many interesting stories, but Celtic religious ritual has no modern relevance—or does it?

Since the late-18th-century Celtic Revival, this culture's myth has inspired output ranging from book series like The Lord of the Rings and A Song of Ice and Fire to their film and television adaptations. Similarly, current religious faiths such as Wicca and causes such as environmentalism have been inspired by our Celtic legacy. Let's explore how below.

The Celtic Revival

During the latter part of the 18th century, a strong interest in Celtic literature, particularly poetry, resulted in the collection of traditional verse and music. Some of this was undertaken by a group of Welshmen, including the harper Edward Jones, who published two collections: The Musical and Poetical Relics of the Welsh Bards (1784) and The Bardic Museum of Primitive Literature of 1802 (Green, 1997). Owen Jones also gathered material about Brittonic cultures in Wales and Charles O'Connor did the same concerning ancient Gaelic traditions in Ireland.

The publication of such materials fueled interest in the ancient Celts. One person who capitalized on this was the Welsh antiquarian and author Iolo Morganwg, who founded the Gorsedd. This society of Welsh-language poets, writers, and musicians later led to the creation of the Neo-Druidism movement.

Morganwg was born Edward Williams in Glamorgan, Wales in 1747. While working as a stonemason in London in the early 1770s, he became involved with other expatriate Welshmen who were concerned that the language and culture of their home country were being lost. Inspired by them, Williams became a bard and assumed the name Iolo Morganwg (Iolo of Glamorgan). Not content to foster modern Welsh culture, he went as far as to invent a pedigree for the bardic tradition in which the Glamorganshire bards belonged to an unbroken tradition stretching back to the ancient Celtic Druids.

While Iolo's scholarship was later found to be fraudulent, his findings were celebrated by his contemporaries. According to the poem "Madoc" written by Robert Southey in the 1820s: "Iolo, old Iolo, he who knows / The virtues of all herbs of mount-vale... / Whatever lore of science or of song / Sages and bards of old have handed down" (Green, 1997: 153).

The Scottish also began to show an increased interest in their Celtic past. Intrigue with the country's Gaelic culture increased during the Romantic period of the late 18th century. Some examples include the novels of Sir Walter Scott and the lyrics and poetry of Thomas Moore.

Inspired by the Romantic movement, this renewed investment in learning more about ancient culture was part of a trend of the revived popularity of folklore, folk tales, and folk music that was occurring more generally in Europe at this time. For example, Beethoven was commissioned to produce a set of arrangements of Scottish folk songs (Castle, 2001). This new appreciation of ancestral identity encouraged and resulted from a growing sense of nationalism throughout Britain, especially in Ireland.

The Celtic Revival continued throughout the 19th century. In the mid-1800s, Sir Samuel Ferguson and the Young Ireland Movement popularized folk tales and histories of countries and territories with Celtic roots. Around the same time, interest in ornamental Celtic art also developed with the increased use of Celtic motifs in the decoration of accessories. Celtic-style jewelry has been popular from the 1840s onward and was inspired by archaeological finds. Scottish and Irish jewelers who excelled at creating reproductions of eighth-century Celtic body ornaments were responsible for its popularization (Campbell, 2006).

The effort to revive ancient Scottish myths and history as inspiration for modern art and prose culminated with the formation of the Edinburgh Social Union in 1885. The organization was similar to factions founded in Ireland around the same time and included several significant figures in the Arts and Crafts and aesthetic movements (Gardiner, 2005). Dundee was a major center of the movement in Scotland, as it was home to key Celtic Revival artists such as John Duncan and Stewart Carmichael and the publisher Malcolm C. MacLeod.

The Irish Literary Revival also celebrated Celtic culture. This renaissance encouraged the creation of works that differentiated Irish culture from its English counterpart, feeding a growing national identity that was also inspired by Irish history, myths, and folklore. In 1892, Sir Charles Gavan Duffy explained (Castle, 2001: 239):

> A group of young men, among the most generous and disinterested in our annals, were busy digging up the buried relics of our history, to enlighten the present by a knowledge of the past, setting up on their pedestals anew the overthrown statues of Irish worthies, assailing wrongs which under long impunity had become unquestioned and even venerable, and warming as with strong wine the heart of the people, by songs of valour and hope; and happily not standing isolated in their pious work, but encouraged and sustained by just such an army of students and sympathizers as I see here to-day.

Examples include writers such as George William Russell, W. B. Yeats, his brother and artist Jack B. Yeats, and J. M. Synge. The three playwrights mentioned all wrote dramas about Deirdre of the Sorrows in the early 1900s. These were Deirdre (1902) by Russell, Deirdre (1907) by Yeats, and Deirdre of the Sorrows (1910) by Synge. These and other works by early 20th-century Irish playwrights reintroduced audiences to the Celtic culture. The poem "The Celtic Twilight" (1893) by the Irish poet, mystic, and visionary W. B. Yeats is an important example of the elevation of folkloric stories to literary status in the Anglo-Irish tradition. The literary and artistic output of Yeats and his fellow countrymen represents the continuity of storytelling and the written word as creative expression in Irish culture to the present day.

Inspiration for Contemporary Literature

Celtic culture, myth, and legend have inspired a great deal of contemporary fantasy literature. One of the most famous examples is J. R. R. Tolkien's Lord of the Rings series, although the author denied that the Arthurian legends influenced him. However, there are indications that he was inspired by ancient Wales. For one, he disliked the Old Irish and Scottish Gaelic tongues, but he claimed to like the Welsh language. He believed that because Welsh was the vernacular of Britain before the Anglo-Saxons—later to become the English—arrived, it conveyed a sense of magic and beauty, evoking an idea of what the land was like before its culture was quashed by invading forces. This implies that early Welsh culture, myth, and legend inspired the writer's novels.

Depictions of the Elves that populate Middle-earth in Lord of the Rings may have been inspired by the Tuatha Dé Danann of Irish Celtic mythology. The exile of the Noldor clan of Elves in The Silmarillion (1977) parallels the story of the mythological race of semi-divine beings who invaded Ireland from across the seas, burning the current inhabitants' ships and fighting them when they arrived. Similarly, the Noldor came to Middle-earth from Valinor, destroyed their vessels, and focused on fighting the Dark Lord, Melkor (Fimi, 2006).

The Elves' sanctuary of Rivendell and the other Elvish realm of Lothlórien parallel Tír na nÓg, the Celtic Otherworld. Like the latter, these domains are hard to find and can only be accessed by crossing a river. This symbolizes the spiritual boundary between the mortal and the immortal. In Rivendell, it is said that "the weary adventurer is transported into a haven of Elven hospitality and delight" (Burns, 2005: 54). Also, the name contains the words "Riven" and "dell," terms suggestive of a low place into which the traveler must descend. Such a downward journey is characteristic of Celtic tales of entry to the Otherworld, which is often depicted as being underground.

The Lord of the Rings is not the only example of contemporary fantasy literature that has or may have been inspired by Celtic myth and legend. Out of many others, Kenneth Morris's The Fates of the Princes of Dyfed (1914) is a retelling of the story of Pwyll, Rhiannon, and Pryderi that comes from the first branch of the Mabinogi. Rhiannon was the Welsh horse goddess turned queen and bestower of sovereignty, Pwyll was her husband, and Pryderi was their son. The sequel to this story was Book of the Three Dragons (1930), a continuation of the former tale but with some changes and adaptations from other branches as well as content that was the author's invention.

Other, more recent examples use mythological material to inspire plots set in the present day. For example, in The Owl Service (1967), Alan Garner portrays a mythic story from the Mabinogion recreating itself tragically in the relationship between two modern families, one English and the other Welsh. Similarly, in his Albion trilogy, Gog (1967), Magog (1972), and King Ludd (1988), Iain Sinclair recreates in modern times what is seen as the ancient struggle between two primal giants at work in British history, Gog, the fugitive spirit of old Britain and Magog, the ruthless entrepreneurial invader. The pattern of these stories reflects folklore and Shakespeare's play King Lear, with the rightful son cast out or marginalized by the illegitimate or half-brother.

These examples suggest that Celtic myth inspires classic plots that can fuel both fantasy tales and also stories about the modern world.

Influence on Popular Culture

Celtic mythology has influenced recent cultural output, such as novels, TV series, films, and video games, including the Disney/Pixar film Brave (2012) and the television series A Game of Thrones (2011–2019) inspired by A Song of Ice and Fire, the series of novels by George R. R. Martin.

Brave

The children's film Brave is set in medieval Scotland and tells the story of young Princess Merida of the Celt clan DunBroch. It has been proposed that the plot is a parable of a maiden's initiation into womanhood. Princess Merida rejects the role prescribed to her by her mother, Queen Elinor, and instead seeks guidance from the previous generation by befriending a witch (a crone-trickster figure). Although she does not trick Merida, granting the protagonist's wish leads the young woman into danger. Merida's mother also learns a difficult lesson. However, during the film, both Elinor and her daughter transform and redefine their roles and their relationship with each other, eventually reconciling and forging conceptualizations of womanhood that are more suitable to their characters (Brundige, 2012).

In this sense, the film utilizes the Celtic tripartite goddess figure of the maiden, mother, and crone, as seen in depictions of the Matres or the goddess Brigid. There is also a hint of The Morrígan, who can transform herself into a crow or a raven. Another figure from Celtic mythology present in the film is the she-bear. Bear goddesses existed in the Celtic world, such as Artio and Andarta, and had parallels with the Greek goddess Artemis, who could take the form of this creature. Furthermore, in Northern Europe, the animal was associated with transformation and shape-changing (Stewart, 1992).

A Game of Thrones

Celtic myth and legend have also influenced George R. R. Martin's series of fantasy novels that inspired the hit television series, A Game of Thrones. His work was inspired by British medieval history and also Celtic myth. The events depicted in the show have parallels with Geoffrey of Monmouth's History of the Kings of Britain (see Chapter 4 for background). For example, in the fictional world, the First Men whose ancestors still populate the North in Westeros and worship the old gods occupy a similar position to that of the Celts in the early medieval world. Notably, trees such as the oak and yew are sacred to the original human inhabitants of the imagined world in the same way they were for the Celts.

Incestuous sexual relationships and the transformation of people into animals occur in both A Game of Thrones and A Song of Ice and Fire. In the series, the character Joffery is the result of an incestuous relationship between his mother and uncle. Similarly, the Celtic myth of Arianhrod says that her two sons were fathered by her brother, Gwydion. In the series, several characters can transform into nearby animals. In the same way, The Morrígan often turns herself into a crow or raven, while Ceridwen also frequently transforms into other creatures.

Perhaps the most obvious aspect of Martin's fictional tale that has been inspired by Celtic myth is the character Brandon "Bran" Stark, who is a version of the Welsh mythological figure Brân the Blessed (or Bendigeidfran as he is known in the Mabinogi). In the series, Bran is the second youngest son of the Stark family and has a special relationship with ravens. Significantly, his name means "raven" in Welsh and the bird is the symbol of the mythical giant. Both figures become kings who have psychic powers and weaknesses in their legs. Also, the story of Brân the Blessed's head having been carried around Britain is reworked, with Bran Stark destined to spend his whole life under the white Weirwood trees, defending Westeros from invaders.

Modern Manifestations

Beyond fiction, Celtic culture has prominent manifestations in the modern world. Notably, many facets of neo-paganism and Wicca have their roots in Celtic mythology.

Neo-Paganism

Contemporary paganism, known as modern or neo-paganism, is a religion or group of religions inspired by the historical beliefs of pre-Christian people living in Europe and nearby areas of North Africa and the Near East. Modern iterations mostly date back to the 1960s and 1970s, and their emergence was connected to the counterculture of that time. These movements share many similarities but are diverse and do not share a single set of practices, beliefs, or texts.

The various religions often rely on pre-Christian, ethnographic, and folkloric sources to inform their beliefs and ritual behavior. Some follow a spiritual path that they accept is entirely modern while others claim to adhere to ancient beliefs or attempt to recreate bygone traditions as accurately as possible. For example, some variants like Heathenry in Germany or Hellenism in Greece seek to mirror the original practices on which they are based as far as possible. Meanwhile, others are more eclectic, blending elements of historical belief systems with other religions and philosophies. Examples of the second approach include Wicca, Druidry, and the Goddess movement. Feminism's influence on Wicca also led to the creation of a subset of the tradition, a goddess-worshiping movement called Dianic Wicca (Adler, 2006).

Interestingly, many neo-pagan movements are secular rather than religious in their philosophies and beliefs. Modern Druidry is a prime example of paganism and how it can exist alongside an atheist or agnostic worldview. Its adherents worship the earth. To them, all life is sacred and worthy of protection. Their view is that there is no heaven as such; rather, they are completely tied to earthly existence. Druidry prides itself on building bridges between faiths, as its followers respect and embrace all religious views, whether Christian, pagan, or undecided.

Public awareness of the neo-pagan movement increased with the publication of books such as Margot Adler's Drawing Down the Moon (1979) and Starhawk's The Spiral Dance (1979). An increasing interest in serious academic research into paganism arose in the 1980s and 1990s. One example is Miranda Green's book Exploring the World of the Druids (1997), which tells the story of the Druids and their involvement in the Celtic tradition from ancient times to the present day. The creation and growth of the internet in the 1990s also expanded the membership and reach of neo-pagan movements.

Paganism is a growing and evolving religion. One example of this is the phenomenon of "fire spinning." This practice was unknown in the 1980s but has since become popular on the pagan festival circuit and is now a staple of these events. Similarly, drumming is a ritual that has emerged in modern times rather than having an ancient precedent.

Wicca

Wicca is a modern mystery religion with a strong emphasis on divine forces and the power of feminine energy. Its followers believe in an all-powerful earth goddess and other nature deities, such as the Horned God.

Wiccan ritual is inspired by the Celtic religion and other alternative spiritual practices such as divination, incantation, dedication, and purification. Its purpose is to "contact the Divine—within and without" (Green, 1997: 164). Rituals mainly focus on the eight seasonal festivals, known as Sabbats. These include the solstices and equinoxes and the four old Celtic seasonal festivals: Imbolc, Beltane, Lughnasadh, and Samhain. These celebrations and other ceremonies often occur outside in the open air so that nature can be venerated.

Celtic Culture as a Source of Inspiration and Celebration

Some contemporary music has drawn inspiration from Celtic myths and culture. One example is the songs and music of Eithne Ní Bhraonáin, popularly known as Enya, which often incorporate elements from Celtic myth and her Irish heritage. The musician grew up in a musical family and felt driven to create unique music and sound from an early age. Most of her songs are self-composed, and the remainder come from Irish tradition. Her first language is Gaelic, and much of her music's lyrics are written in her native tongue.

Her lyrics idealize the Celts by presenting them as a voice of spirituality, nature, and virtue. Her songs refer to aspects of nature, the spiritual journey, and human deeds. They also appear to allude to the journey to the Celtic Otherworld. For example, in her song "May It Be," Enya alludes to a lonely journey: "May it be an evening star / Shines down upon you / May it be when darkness falls / Your heart will be true / You walk a lonely road / Oh, how far you are from home" (Motherway, 2013).

Again, in her song "Only Time," she speaks of a journey, most likely the course of life, where we travel to an unknown and uncertain destination: "Who can say where the road goes? / Where the day flows? Only time / And who can say if your love grows / As your heart chose? Only time."

These lyrics are notable because there were many Otherworlds, so throughout their lives, the Celts could not be certain to which one they would go when they died or even if they might visit there in life.

Enya utilizes technology to create musical arrangements that hark back to the Celtic past. She uses studio techniques to create a sense of distinction in her work that is intended to evoke the effect of the mystical Otherworld. Instruments such as the harp are stimulated to provide an aural reference to Celtic culture. Similarly, the effect of tubular bells is utilized to make aural reference to Celtic paganism. The Celts imagined the Land of Promise as ethereal and apart from the mortal realm, so by creating a similarly transcendental sound, Enya's music evokes this world and its effect.

Technology is also applied to Enya's voice, which it renders otherworldly and mystical. It has been suggested that this tone refers to the ancient Irish practice of keening, a vocal lament for the dead, which makes perfect sense if it is assumed that many of her songs refer to the journey between the mortal realm and the Otherworld.

Enya's image further portrays her as an ethereal presence—seductive yet pure, frail, and distant. This reaffirms her position as a defender of Irish culture against English colonial forces. Her music is popular with the New

Age movement due to their shared values, and her contribution to creating the score for The Lord of the Rings films reaffirms her and Tolkien's links to Celtic culture.

Enya's music is not the only current celebration of Celtic culture today. Festivals like Beltane and Samhain are still celebrated and originated with the ancient Celts. For example, the latter has evolved and is now widely celebrated as Halloween. Also, pagans and New Age believers still celebrate and revere ancient Celtic festivals.

Applying Ancient Mythological Wisdom to Contemporary Life

Mythology delves into the human psyche. By exploring archetypes, symbols, and the struggle of heroes, myths provide insights into our emotions, fears, and desires. Jungian analysis and modern feminist interpretations of psychological understanding found in myths show how these stories can help people navigate their inner worlds. Clarissa Pinkola Estes (1992: 20) explains that:

> Stories set the inner life into motion, and this is particularly important where the inner life is frightened, wedged, or cornered. Story greases the hoists and pulleys, it causes adrenaline to surge, shows us the way out, down, or up, and for our trouble, cuts for us fine wide doors in previously blank walls, openings that lead to the dreamland, that lead to love and learning.

Celtic myth and legend can teach us about courage and loyalty. The hero Cú Chulainn is remembered for his embodiment of these qualities. In "The Táin," the hero agrees to fight for Ulster against the forces of Queen Medb of Connacht. As all the other men in Ulster are under a curse that means that they cannot participate in protecting their land at the time, he must complete the defense of his land with no support.

It is a testament to his courage that Cú Chulainn does so and to his loyalty that he does not abandon his fellow Ulstermen. Even when the goddess The Morrígan appears to him as a beautiful maiden and tries to seduce him, the young warrior remains faithful to his kingdom. His bravery and devotion mean that his example remains relevant today. Furthermore, before his death, he was also a man who was strong enough to do the right thing and remained faithful in the face of temptation. These attributes make him a role model and a symbol of positive masculinity that is relevant today.

Celtic Mythology and Modern Issues

Druidry is an example of a modern Celtic religion that applies Celtic values, such as the veneration of the past and a respect for nature, to modern issues. First, the practice promotes a strong belief in a link between the present and the remote past. One example is its emphasis on the sacred function of ancient stone circles like Stonehenge. From the late 19th century onward, Druidic groups have used this site on ceremonial occasions, particularly during the summer and winter solstices. The rituals they perform are a combination of ancient religion and invention.

Stonehenge in particular continues to be a focus of Druidic rituals, especially on Midsummer Day. Since the early 1970s, at the summer solstice, the Druids have kept a midnight vigil at the disc barrow on Normanton Down, followed by a long predawn ceremony at Stonehenge, culminating in the blowing of bronze horns to greet the first light of Midsummer Day.

The authorities have sometimes prevented the Druids from accessing the site to perform their rituals. Following several instances where trespassers broke in and vandalized the ancient stones in the 1960s, barbed wire fences were put up to protect the monuments. The introduction of the Criminal Justice Act in the 1990s curtailed the gathering of large Druid groups there as well. Followers of the religion argue that this is unjust, as no other faith group was prevented from entering sacred sites to carry out their rituals. Since then, Open Access Events where everyone can access the site have been introduced during solstices and equinoxes.

Like modern Druids, the Celts revered the past, as demonstrated by the commitment of their bards to remembering numerous stories, myths, and legends about their past. As the ancient Druids believed that religious knowledge was too sacred to be written down, they had to remember these facts and transmit them orally from generation to generation. The challenge in this is evidenced in "The Táin," where we find out that at one point the Chief Poet of Ireland called together a council of bards because the full story of the famous cattle raid was no longer known. It was only when a young poet named Muirgen sat at the grave of the great poet Fergus mac Róich and his spirit transmitted the full story to the living man that the Celts regained their knowledge of what had occurred.

To fulfill the path of the Druid, the individual must seek a deeper under-standing of nature, the planet, and themselves. This focus has led many of those involved in the neo-pagan movement to become environmentalists. For example, all modern Druids are deeply committed to conservationism. This reflects the values of the Celts, whose reverence of nature and view of it as sacred is reflected in their belief in animism, the concept that all living things have a soul. This meant that they were committed to the reverence and protection of the natural world.

Summary

Although the Celtic religion died out after the advent of Christianity, its myths and legends are so appealing and compelling that they have survived in some form ever since. First written down in the Middle Ages, these stories survive into the present day, although perhaps not in their original form. Their appeal led to the Celtic Revival gaining momentum from the late-18th century onward. Today, a great deal of cultural output from the music of Enya to The Lord of the Rings to A Game of Thrones owes something to the Celtic past. The Celts have even shown us how to navigate our fears about the current state of the environment.

As we are nearing the end of this guide, an understanding of Celtic myth and legend and why it is relevant today will be summed up in the final chapter.

Chapter Six

Conclusion

May it be the shadow's call will fly away
May it be your journey on to light the day
When the night is overcome
You may rise to find the sun.

– Enya, from "May It Be"

This *Beginners Guide to Celtic Mythology* has introduced the key gods, deities, characters, stories, themes, and mythological cycles found in Celtic myth. It also aimed to explain how to understand these stories and looked at how other cultures, such as Roman, Norse, Christian, and Arthurian, either influenced or informed the Celts and their beliefs. Finally, we considered how Celtic mythology continues to influence us today.

We have addressed that myths have occurred in all cultures and societies throughout human history. In his book *The Power of Myth*, Joseph Campbell argues that myths are universally relatable and convey "mankind's one great story" (1988: 64). The reappearance of certain themes time and again

89

has led us to the realization that these stories portray universal and eternal truths about humanity. While we have focused on Celtic myth in this book, we have also explored the ubiquitous nature of the lessons these tales seek to convey.

Through these teachings, mythology and folklore serve other important functions. Psychological studies about storytelling and human nature tell us that the brain uses narratives as a way of assessing risk and planning for the future. By learning the rules of the world and simulating outcomes for decision-making, the mind can play out events without the risk and exposure of attempting them physically (Gottschall, 2012). As Celtic myths and other mythological stories allow us to explore scenarios without enacting them, they are still appealing today.

Major Themes

One key function of myth is to understand and accept birth, growth, and death (Campbell, 1988). An example of this can be found in Celtic mythology in the interactions between the hero Cú Chulainn and The Morrígan in "The Táin." The goddess appears several times to the hero as a femme fatale figure, initially as a lovely young girl who wants to make love to him, then in several different animal forms. However, she fails to seduce him in each instance. Instead, he fights and injures her. Later, she appears to him as an old milch cow and, as she allows him to drink from her, tells him of his death. Once he has died in battle, she hovers over him in the form of a crow.

The Morrígan's role in "The Táin" is to impart her wisdom about the cycle of life to Cú Chulainn. By doing so, she explains to him that, while he may be a powerful hero now, he will not remain so forever, as everyone is subject to the cycle of life. We will all be born and we all, however gifted, talented, and wonderful we may be, will eventually die.

Themes such as the life-death-rebirth cycle are universal to all world mythologies. Other motifs that make Celtic mythology special include animal symbolism, magic and enchantment, and heroes and monsters. One significant recurrence is power female figures. Women were valued in Celtic society, had sexual and personal freedom, and could assume male roles, such as those of rulers or warriors if they so wished. Such female dominance and autonomy find their way into Celtic myth in the form of characters such as the powerful and sexually empowered Queen Medb of Connacht, The Morrígan, and the warrior sisters Scáthach and Aífe.

Other themes such as magic, heroes, and monsters often appear in Celtic myth. One example is the enchantment Macha places the men of Ulster under in "The Táin," which means that no man but Cú Chulainn can fight against the forces of Connacht. Celtic mythological monsters include the banshee and leprechauns, both of which evolved from old stories. These common subjects influence modern cultural output, as they can be found in Celtic-inspired stories such as The Lord of the Rings series of books and films or A Song of Ice and Fire and its television adaptation, *A Game of Thrones*.

History, Mythology, and Interpretation

Interpretations of Celtic mythology over time have been influenced by major historical events, especially the advent of Christianity in Europe. While Celtic stories and legends survived the introduction of a new religious doctrine, they were likely altered to turn gods into mortals or, in some cases, like Lugh, into magical beings like leprechauns. Although Christian scribes can be credited with writing down Celtic myths, ensuring that they survived the test of time, they also changed many important details.

Other cases also suggest that Celtic myth may have been recorded in a way that combined historical events with lore and legend. A prime example is the figure of King Arthur. There is some evidence that suggests that he was a real historical figure, a Romano-Celtic commander living before the sixth century C.E. Alternative sources indicate that he was based on a minor Celtic deity. It could be that these real and imagined personages came together to eventually create a new body of myth: the Arthurian Legends.

Breathing Life Into Ancient Wisdom

In the words of W. B. Yeats, "The world is full of magic things, patiently waiting for our senses to grow sharper."

The stories and symbols in Celtic mythology carry deep meanings about life, nature, and the human spirit. The myths constantly remind us that, despite our efforts to impose order on life, it remains elusive and mysterious. Yet it is that very enigma that offers us a sliver of light in the darkness of the constraints imposed upon us. These tales aren't just ancient history—they contain living wisdom. Here are just a few examples of the practical application of these insights.

The first lesson we can apply from Celtic mythology to our lives today is a profound respect for nature. The Celts understood that we are not separate from our landscapes and their creatures, nor are we superior to them. Rather, we are intrinsically part of the earth. Attempts to dominate it can only lead to our destruction. We cannot harm this planet that we call home without hurting ourselves. It is vital at this time of environmental crisis that we strengthen our bond with the living world and acknowledge the interconnectedness between ourselves and the natural world.

Another powerful theme in Celtic mythology that we can incorporate into daily living is the concept of shape-shifting. Many characters in the tales presented in this book could transform themselves into animals or other elements of nature. We could interpret this as symbolic of the need to remain open and adaptable. Although we may struggle with accepting change, it is an inevitable part of life. Rather than resist it, rock-like, we increase our resilience if we can shift into a body of flowing water when circumstances demand it. All change, however difficult, is an opportunity for growth and transformation.

The symbol of the Celtic knot, a loop without a beginning or end, is another reminder of the eternal cycle of rebirth. This ties into the lesson that Celtic mythology offers us regarding death and renewal, which may be a particularly difficult one to apply. Our time on this earth is short, and we must make the most of it. All life eventually comes to an end, yet the Celtic view of life as cyclical rather than finite and of death as a mere change of state in a natural and constant process of revival offers comfort and hope.

The importance of courage and heroism is another timeless lesson that never loses its relevance. The heroes in these tales, regardless of their gender, faced daunting, seemingly insurmountable challenges, yet they persevered with bravery and determination. Mythology serves to remind us that we, too, have the inner strength to overcome our obstacles. Every human being is the hero of their quest, as they journey through life, battling inner and outer demons. It takes courage simply to live, yet Celtic mythology demonstrates how we are supplied with mysterious resources that guide us and guard us.

In closing, let us take with us the words of the poem "Beannacht/Blessing" by John O'Donohue:

> May the nourishment of the earth be yours,
> may the clarity of light be yours,
> may the fluency of the ocean be yours,
> may the protection of the ancestors be yours.
> And so may a slow
> wind work these words
> of love around you,
> an invisible cloak
> to mind your life.

If you have enjoyed reading this book, it would be greatly appreciated if you would take a moment to give it a quick review and rating on Amazon. This is so helpful in boosting its visibility.

To make this quick and easy for you, just scan the QR code of your country's marketplace to take you straight to the 'leave a review' section.

Many thanks again for choosing to read this book, and please keep your eye out for upcoming books in this series.

www.nevesullivan.com

US: To leave a review on amazon.com:

UK: To leave a review on amazon.co.uk:

Australia: To leave a review on amazon.com.au:

Canada: To leave a review on amazon.ca:

Chapter Seven

Glossary of Terms Related to Celtic History and Culture

Alba: Celtic Irish name for Scotland.

Animism: The belief that all living things, including plants and natural phenomena, have souls.

Awen: In Welsh lore, this word means wisdom, prophecy, and inspiration.

Druid: Celtic priests who led worship, law, politics, and society in the Celtic world.

Gaelic: This was the Celtic language and culture of Scotland and sometimes Ireland.

Gaul/Gauls/Gallic: Roman name for modern-day France.

Gorsedd: A society of Welsh language poets, writers, musicians, and others who promote Welsh culture. It was founded by Iolo Morganwg in the 18th century.

Iron Age: The final pre-historical age that began in around 1200 B.C.E. and ended in around 550 B.C.E.

Keening: Irish vocal lament for the dead.

Mabinogi: Earliest Welsh prose stories compiled in Middle Welsh between the 12th and 13th centuries C.E. The text is also the source of much of what we know about Celtic mythology.

Neo-paganism: The body of modern or contemporary pagan traditions based on ancient or reimagined pagan beliefs.

Ogham: The Celtic tree alphabet consisting of 20 trees or symbols.

Pantheon: The family or tradition groups of gods and goddesses belong to.

The Táin: The shortened name of the famous story, "Táin Bó Cúailnge," or "The Cattle Raid of Cooley." This is perhaps the most famous Irish Celtic myth and tells us a lot about Celtic history and culture.

Tuatha Dé Danann: A supernatural race that many of the Irish gods and goddesses belonged to and that lived in Ireland in ancient times.

About the Author

Neve Sullivan holds a BA Honors degree and a postgraduate diploma, with her dissertation focusing on Irish cultural identity through the arts: literature, poetry, song, and painting. Neve worked in libraries and archives for many years, further deepening her understanding and appreciation of historical texts.

Neve's travels and her fascination with different cultures has greatly influenced her writing style and content. Her love for nature is also evident in her work, as she often explores the connection between spirituality and the natural world.

Through her series *Celtic Wisdom for Modern Life*, Neve aims to help readers ease their contemporary, fractured alienation from our collective past and our ancestral roots. Her goal is to foster a sense of continuity with history while aiding readers in reconnecting with ancient Celtic wisdom and discovering a new reverence for nature and the arts. To learn more about Neve's books please scan the QR code below or visit www.neves ullivan.com

ALSO BY

Neve Sullivan

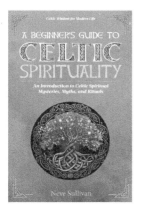 A Beginner's Guide to Celtic Spirituality: An Introduction to Celtic Spiritual Mysteries, Myths, and Rituals

Coming soon:

A Beginner's Guide to Greek Mythology: An introduction to the gods and goddesses, mythical creatures and muses of ancient Greece

www.nevesullivan.com

CHAPTER EIGHT

REFERENCES & BIBLIOGRAPHY

Abram, C. (2011). *Myths of the pagan north: The god of the Norsemen.* Continuum.

Adler, M. (2006). *Drawing down the moon: Witches, druids.* Penguin.

Alberro, M. (2005). Celtic legacy in Galicia. *E-Keltoi: Journal of Interdisciplinary Celtic Studies, 6:* 1005–1035.

Alcock, J. (2011). *Roman Britain: Conquest and civilization.* Hatchette.

Anderson, E. N. (2014). *Caring for place: Ecology, ideology, and emotion in traditional landscape management.* Routledge.

Andren, A. (2011). Old Norse and Germanic religion. In T. Insoll, (Ed.), *The Oxford handbook of the archaeology of ritual and religion.* Oxford University Press.

Asher, H. (2023, November 4). *The importance of nature connection in Celtic culture: Exploring animism and Celtic beliefs.* An Darach. https://silvotherapy.co.uk/articles/nature-connection-celts

Bane, T. (2020). *Encyclopedia of mythological objects.* McFarland & Company.

Barber, N. (2014). *The way they never were: Nationalism, landscape, and the myth in Irish identity construction.* [Master of Arts thesis, Georgia

State University]. ScholarWorks @ Georgia State University. https://sc holarworks.gsu.edu/rs_theses/47/

Berg, S. (2022). *Brigid: The Celtic goddess who became a saint*. Creek Ridge Publishing.

Blair, P. H. (2003). *An introduction to Anglo-Saxon England* (3rd ed.). Cambridge University Press.

Brundige, E. (2012, June 12). *Brave: "The bear and the bow:" Bear mythology*.
Mythpile. http://www.mythphile.com/2012/06/brave-the-bear-and-t he-bow/

Burkeman, O. (2014). This column will change your life: Where Heaven and Earth collide. *The Guardian*. https://www.theguardian.com/lifea ndstyle/2014/mar/22/this-column-change-your-life-heaven-earth

Burns, M. (2005). *Perilous realms: Celtic and Norse in Tolkien's Middle-earth*. University of Toronto Press.

Byghan, Y. (2020). *Sacred and mythological animals: A worldwide taxonomy*. McFarland & Company.

Campbell, J. (1988). *The power of myth*. Anchor Books.

Campbell, J. (2004). *Bede [St Bede, Baeda, known as the Venerable Bede] (673/4-735)*. Oxford Dictionary of National Biography.
https://www.oxforddnb.com/display/10.1093/ref:odnb/978019861412 8.001.0001/odnb-9780198614128-e-1922

Campbell, G. (Ed.). (2006). *The Grove encyclopedia of decorative arts*. Oxford University Press.

Carpenter, D. D. (1996). Emergent nature spirituality: An examination of the major spiritual contours of the contemporary pagan worldview. In J.R. Lewis (Ed.). *Magical religion and modern witchcraft*. State University of New York Press.

Cartwright, M. (2021a). *The ancient Celtic pantheon*.
World History Encyclopedia.
https://www.worldhistory.org/article/1715/the-ancient-celtic-pantheon/

Cartwright, M. (2021b). *Death, burial, and the afterlife in ancient Celtic religion. Brewminate*.

https://brewminate.com/death-burial-and-the-afterlife-in-ancient-celtic-religion/

Castle, G. (2001). *Modernism and the Celtic revival*. Cambridge University Press.

Chadwick, H. M. (1900). The oak and the thunder-god. *The Journal of the Anthropological Institute of Great Britain and Ireland, 30*: 22–44.

Chadwick, N. K. (1960). *The age of the saints in the early Celtic church*. Llanerch Publishers.

Chadwick, N. K. (1970). *The Celts*. Penguin.

Condren, M. (1989). *The serpent and the goddess: Women, religion, and power in Celtic Ireland*. Harper & Row.

Coney, B. (2021). The guide to getting into Enya, patron saint of mystical mood music.

Vice. https://www.vice.com/en/article/epnnyn/the-guide-to-getting-into-enya-patron-saint-of-mystical-mood-music

Cunliffe B. (1997). *The ancient Celts*. Oxford University Press.

Cusack, C. M. (1998). *Conversion among the Germanic peoples*. Cassell.

Davidson, H. R. E. (1964). *Gods and myths of northern Europe*. Penguin.

Davidson, H. R. E. (1988). *Myth and symbols in pagan Europe: Early Scandinavian and Celtic religions*. Manchester University Press.

De Camp, L. S. (1964). *Citadels of mystery*. Fontana.

Depuis, N. (2009). *Mna na hEireann: Women who shaped Ireland*. Mercier Press.

The Editors of Encyclopaedia Britannica. (2024a). *Brigit: Celtic deity*. Britannica. https://www.britannica.com/topic/Brigit

The Editors of Encyclopaedia Britannica. (2024b). *The cattle raid of Cooley*.
Britannica. https://www.britannica.com/topic/The-Cattle-Raid-of-Cooley

The Editors of Encyclopaedia Britannica. (2024c). *Bran*. Britannica https://www.britannica.com/topic/Bran-Celtic-god

Ellis, P. B. (1987). *A dictionary of Irish mythology*. Constable.

Ellis, P. B. (1999). *The Chronicles of the Celts: New tellings of their myths & legends*. Carroll & Graf Publishers, Inc.

Ellis, P. B. (2002). *The mammoth book of Celtic myths and legends*. Constable & Robinson Ltd.

Estes, C. P. (1992). *Women who run with the wolves: Contacting the power of the wild woman*. Rider.

Eyres, K. (2007). *Celtic myth*. Flame Tree Publishing.

Falkner, D. E. (2020). *The mythology of the night sky: Greek, Roman, and other celestial lore* (2nd ed.). Springer.

Farmer, D. H. (1978). *The Oxford dictionary of saints*. Oxford University Press.

Fimi, D. (2006). *"Mad" elves and "elusive beauty": Some Celtic strands of Tolkien's mythology*. Dr Dimitra Fimi. http://dimitrafimi.com/mad-elves-and-elusive-beauty-some-celtic-strands-of-tolkiens-mythology/

Fimi, D. (2010). *Tolkien, race, and cultural history: From fairies to hobbits*. Palgrave.

Ford, P. K. (1996). Prolegomena to a reading of the *Mabinogi*: "Pwyll" and "Manawydan." In C.W. Sullivan (Ed.). *The Mabinogi: A book of essays*. Garland Publishing, Inc.

Freeman, P. (2021). *Celtic spirituality: An introduction to the sacred wisdom of the Celts*. St Martin's Publishing Group.

Frye, N. (1963). *Fables of identity*. Harcourt, Brace.

Gardiner, M. (2005). *Modern Scottish culture*. Edinburgh University Press.

Geoffrey of Monmouth. (1966). *The history of the kings of Britain* (L. Thorpe., Trans.). Penguin.

Gottschall, J. (2012). *The storytelling animal: How stories make us human*. Houghton Mifflin Harcourt.

Grace, R. (2024). *The children of Lir*. Irish Jewelry Craft. https://www.irishjewelrycraft.com/blog/irish-culture/the-children-of-lir

Green, M. (1989). *Symbol & image in Celtic religious art*. Routledge.

Green, M. (1992). *Animals in Celtic life and myth*. Routledge.

Green, M. (1996). *Celtic art: Symbols & imagery*. Sterling Publishing Co., Inc.

Green, M. J. (1997). *Exploring the world of the Druids*. Thames & Hudson.

Grigsby, J. (2002). *Warriors of the wasteland*. Watkins.

Heinz, S. (1997). *Celtic symbols*. Sterling Publishing Company, Inc.

Heinz, S. (2010). Afterlife and Celtic concepts of the otherworld. In L. Sikorska (Ed.), *Thise stories beren witnesse: The landscape of the afterlife in medieval and post-medieval imagination.* Peter Lang.

Hilliard, P. C. (2014). Quae res quem sit habitura finem, posterior aestas videbit: Prosperity, adversity, and Bede's hope for the future of Northumbria. In P. Darby, & Wallis, F. (Eds.), *Bede and the future.* Routledge.

Horwood, G. (2008). *Tai Chi Chuan and the code of life: Revealing the deeper mysteries of China's ancient art for health and harmony, revised edition.* Dragon Door Publications.

Irby-Massie, G. L. (1999). *Military religion in Roman Britain.* Brill.

Jadhav, S. (2019, February 10). *To be Enya, is an art.* Medium. https://speedeaglesj.medium.com/to-be-enya-is-an-art-162de8904d75

Jarron, M. (2015). *"Independent and individualist": Art in Dundee 1867–1924.* Abertay Historical Society.

Jenkins, E. (1990). *The mystery of Arthur.* Michael O'Mara.

Jesch, J. (2011). The Norse gods in England and the Isle of Man. In D. Anlezark (Ed.), *Myths, legends, and heroes: Essays on Old Norse and Old English literature.* University of Toronto Press.

Jolly, K. L. (1996). *Popular religion in late Saxon England: Elf charms in context.* University of North Carolina Press.

Jones, I. M. (2017). *5 parallels between Game of Thrones and Welsh mythology.* Nation Cymru. https://nation.cymru/opinion/5-parallels-between-game-of-thrones-and-welsh-mythology/

King, A. (1990). *Roman Gaul and Germany.* The University of California Press.

Klimczak, N. (2016). *Female Druids, the forgotten priestesses of the Celts.* Ancient Origins. https://www.ancient-origins.net/history/female-druids-forgotten-priestesses-celts-005910

Koch, J. (2006). *Celtic culture: A historical encyclopedia.* ABC–CLIO.

Koch, J. T., & Minard, A. (Eds.). (2012). *The Celts: History, life, and culture, Vol. 1.* ABC–CLIO.

Leslie, C. W., & Gerace, F. E. (2000). *The ancient Celtic festivals and how we celebrate them today*. Simon & Schuster.

Leviton, R. (2006). *The gods in their cities: Geomantic locales of the ray masters and great white brotherhood, and how to interact with them*. iUniverse, Inc.

Mac Cana, P. (1985). *Celtic mythology: Revised edition*. Peter Bedrick Books.

MacCulloch, J. A. (1911). *The religion of the ancient Celts*. T&T Clark.

MacDonald, M. (2000). *Scottish art*. Thames and Hudson.

MacEowen, F. (2007). *The Celtic way of seeing: Meditations on the Irish spirit wheel*. New World Library.

MacKillop, J. (1986). *Fionn mac Cumhail: Celtic myth in English literature*. Syracuse University Press.

MacKillop, J. (1998). *Dictionary of Celtic mythology*. Oxford University Press.

Magan, M. (2017). *Fairy forts: Why these "sacred places" deserve our respect*. The Irish Times. https://www.irishtimes.com/culture/heritage/fairy-forts-why-these-sacred-places-deserve-our-respect-1.3181259

Mallory, J. P., & Adams, D. Q. (2006). *The Oxford introduction to Proto-Indo-European and the Proto-Indo-European world*. Oxford University Press.

Mallory, J. P., & Adams, D. Q. (Eds.). (1997). *Encyclopedia of Indo-European culture*. Fitzroy Dearborn Publishers.

Manlove, C. N. (1999). *The fantasy literature of England*. Wipf & Stock.

Marquis, M. (2015). *Beltane: Rituals, recipes, & lore for May Day*. Llewellyn Worldwide.

Matson, G. (2004). *Celtic mythologies A to Z*. Facts on File.

Matthews, R. (2010). *Wales: A very peculiar history*. Book House.

McColman, C. (2003). *The complete idiot's guide to Celtic wisdom*. Alpha.

McCoppin, R. S. (2022). *Goddess lost: How the downfall of female deities downgraded women's status in world cultures*. McFarland & Company.

Meany, A. (1970). AEthelweard, AElfic, the Norse gods, and Northumbria. *Journal of Religious History, 6*(2): 105–132.

Miller, D. A. (1998). On the mythology of Indo-European heroic hair. *Journal of Indo-European Studies, 26*(1-2): 41-60.

Morris, J. (1973). *The age of Arthur: A history of the British Isles from 350 to 650*. Weidenfeld.

Morris, M. (2008). *A great and terrible king: Edward I and the forging of Britain*. Hutchinson.

Motherway, S. H. (2013). *The globalization of Irish traditional song performance*. Routledge.

Murray, E. (2013). *Echoes of an older god? Some notes on Arthur as a pagan deity.* King Arthur in Scotland. https://arthurianscotland.wordpress.com/2013/06/18/echoes-of-an-older-god-some-notes-on-arthur-as-a-pagan-deity-by-eddie-murray/

NicGrioghair, B. (2024). *Bridget, bright goddess of the Gael*. Mythical Ireland. https://mythicalireland.com/blogs/myths-legends/bridget-bright-goddess-of-the-gael

NicMhacha, S. M. (2005). *Queen of the Night: Rediscovering the Celtic moon goddess*. Weiser Books.

O'Giollain, D. (1991). *The good people: New Fairylore essays*. Garland.

O'Hara, K. (2023). *11 major Celtic gods and goddesses*. The Irish Road Trip. https://www.theirishroadtrip.com/celtic-gods-and-goddesses/

Olmsted, G. S. (1976). The Gundestrup version of *Tain Bo Cuailnge*. *Antiquity, 50*(198): 95–103.

O'Neill, E. (2018). *Magic and mystery of Ireland's rivers*. Transceltic. https://www.transceltic.com/irish/magic-and-mystery-of-ireland-s-rivers

Redwine, E. B. (2021). *Gender, performance, and authorship at the Abbey Theatre*. Oxford University Press.

Reginald, R., & Menville, D. (2005). *Classics of fantasy literature: Selected review essays*. Wildside Press.

Richards, J. D. (1991). *Viking age England*. B.T. Batsford.

Roderick, T. (2013). *Wicca: A year and a day: 366 days of spiritual practice in the craft of the wise*. Llewellyn Worldwide.

Rollaston, D. (2003). *Northumbria, 500–1100*. Cambridge University Press.

Ross, A. (1972). *Everyday life of the pagan Celts*. Carousel Books.

Sailor, S. S. (1998). Suibne Geilt: Puzzles, problems, and paradoxes. *The Canadian Journal of Irish Studies*, *24*(1): 115–131.

Sipos, N. (2022). Bran remembers: The narrative process of *A Game of Thrones*. In K. Horvath, J. Mudriczki, & Osztroluczky, S. (Eds.), *Diversity in narration and writing: The novel*. Cambridge Scholars Publishing.

Steele, A. (2023). *12 most famous Norse gods and goddesses*. Smithing Society. https://smithingsociety.com/blacksmithing/history/norse-gods-and-goddesses/

Stewart, R. J. (1992). *Celtic gods, Celtic goddesses*. Cassell Illustrated.

Turville-Petre, E. O. (1975). *Myth and religion of the north: The religion of ancient Scandinavia*. Greenwood Press.

Visit Armagh. (2024). *The curse of Macha*. https://visitarmagh.com/stories/live-our-celtic-myths-legends-in-the-ancient-site-of-navan-fort/the-curse-of-macha/

Waldeman, C., & Mason, C. (2006). *Encyclopedia of European peoples*. Facts On File.

Weber, C. (2015). *Brigid: History, mystery, and magick of the Celtic goddess*. Weiser Books.

Wiley, D. M. (2005). The threefold death. In C. Duffy (Ed.), *Medieval Ireland: An encyclopedia*. Routledge.

Wright, G. (2022). *Ceridwen*. Mythopedia. https://mythopedia.com/topics/ceridwen

Made in the USA
Las Vegas, NV
18 January 2025

16634298R00073